Photo credit: © Jerry Markatos

ABOUT THE AUTHOR

Frederick P. Brooks, Jr., is Kenan Professor of Computer Science at the University of North Carolina at Chapel Hill. He is best known as the "father of the IBM System/360," having served as project manager for its development and later as manager of the Operating System/360 software project during its design phase. For this work he, Bob Evans, and Erich Bloch were awarded the National Medal of Technology in 1985. Earlier, he was an architect of the IBM Stretch and Harvest computers.

At Chapel Hill, Dr. Brooks founded the Department of Computer Science and chaired it from 1964 through 1984. He has served on the National Science Board and the Defense Science Board. His current teaching and research is in computer architecture, molecular graphics, and virtual environments.

The Mythical Man-Month

Essays on Software Engineering

Anniversary Edition

Frederick P. Brooks, Jr.
University of North Carolina at Chapel Hill

ADDISON-WESLEY
An imprint of Addison Wesley Longman, Inc.

Reading, Massachusetts • Harlow, England • Menlo Park, California
Berkeley, California • Don Mills, Ontario • Sydney
Bonn • Amsterdam • Tokyo • Mexico City

Cover drawing: C. R. Knight, Mural of the La Brea Tar Pits. Courtesy of the George C. Page Museum of La Brea Discoveries, The Natural History Museum of Los Angeles County.

The essay entitled, No Silver Bullet, is from Information Processing 1986, the Proceedings of the IFIP Tenth World Computing Conference, edited by H.-J. Kugler, 1986, pages 1069–1076. Reprinted with the kind permission of IFIP and Elsevier Science B.V., Amsterdam, The Netherlands.

Library of Congress Cataloging-in-Publication Data

Brooks, Frederick P., Jr. (Frederick Phillips)
    The mythical man-month : essays on software engineering /
Frederick P. Brooks, Jr. — Anniversary ed.
        p.   cm.
    Includes bibliographical references and index.
    ISBN 0-201-83595-9
    1. Software engineering.   I. Title.
QA76.758.B75   1995
005.1'068—dc20   94-36653
                                                                        CIP

6 7 8 9 10 11-MA-999897

Dedication of the 1975 edition

To two who especially enriched my IBM years:
Thomas J. Watson, Jr.,
whose deep concern for people still permeates his company,
and
Bob O. Evans,
whose bold leadership turned work into adventure.

Dedication of the 1995 edition

To Nancy,
God's gift to me.

Preface to the 20th Anniversary Edition

To my surprise and delight, *The Mythical Man-Month* continues to be popular after 20 years. Over 250,000 copies are in print. People often ask which of the opinions and recommendations set forth in 1975 I still hold, and which have changed, and how. Whereas I have from time to time addressed that question in lectures, I have long wanted to essay it in writing.

Peter Gordon, now a Publishing Partner at Addison-Wesley, has been working with me patiently and helpfully since 1980. He proposed that we prepare an Anniversary Edition. We decided not to revise the original, but to reprint it untouched (except for trivial corrections) and to augment it with more current thoughts.

Chapter 16 reprints "No Silver Bullet: Essence and Accidents of Software Engineering," a 1986 IFIPS paper that grew out of my experience chairing a Defense Science Board study on military software. My coauthors of that study, and our executive secretary, Robert L. Patrick, were invaluable in bringing me back into touch with real-world large software projects. The paper was reprinted in 1987 in the IEEE *Computer* magazine, which gave it wide circulation.

"No Silver Bullet" proved provocative. It predicted that a decade would not see any programming technique that would by itself bring an order-of-magnitude improvement in software productivity. The decade has a year to run; my prediction seems safe. "NSB" has stimulated more and more spirited discussion in the literature than has *The Mythical Man-Month*. Chapter 17, therefore, comments on some of the published critique and updates the opinions set forth in 1986.

In preparing my retrospective and update of *The Mythical Man-Month*, I was struck by how few of the propositions asserted in it have been critiqued, proven, or disproven by ongoing software engineering research and experience. It proved useful to me now to catalog those propositions in raw form, stripped of supporting arguments and data. In hopes that these bald statements will invite arguments and facts to prove, disprove, update, or refine those propositions, I have included this outline as Chapter 18.

Chapter 19 is the updating essay itself. The reader should be warned that the new opinions are not nearly so well informed by experience in the trenches as the original book was. I have been at work in a university, not industry, and on small-scale projects, not large ones. Since 1986, I have only taught software engineering, not done research in it at all. My research has rather been on virtual environments and their applications.

In preparing this retrospective, I have sought the current views of friends who are indeed at work in software engineering. For a wonderful willingness to share views, to comment thoughtfully on drafts, and to re-educate me, I am indebted to Barry Boehm, Ken Brooks, Dick Case, James Coggins, Tom DeMarco, Jim McCarthy, David Parnas, Earl Wheeler, and Edward Yourdon. Fay Ward has superbly handled the technical production of the new chapters.

I thank Gordon Bell, Bruce Buchanan, Rick Hayes-Roth, my colleagues on the Defense Science Board Task Force on Military Software, and, most especially, David Parnas for their insights and stimulating ideas for, and Rebekah Bierly for technical production of, the paper printed here as Chapter 16. Analyzing the software problem into the categories of *essence* and *accident* was inspired by Nancy Greenwood Brooks, who used such analysis in a paper on Suzuki violin pedagogy.

Addison-Wesley's house custom did not permit me to acknowledge in the preface to the 1975 edition the key roles played by their staff. Two persons' contributions should be especially cited: Norman Stanton, then Executive Editor, and Herbert Boes, then Art Director. Boes developed the elegant style, which one reviewer especially cited: "wide margins, [and] imaginative use of typeface and layout." More important, he also made the crucial recommendation that every chapter have an opening picture. (I had only the Tar Pit and Reims Cathedral at the time.) Finding the pictures occasioned an extra year's work for me, but I am eternally grateful for the counsel.

Soli Deo gloria—To God alone be glory.

Chapel Hill, N.C.   F. P. B., Jr.
March 1995

Preface to the First Edition

In many ways, managing a large computer programming project is like managing any other large undertaking—in more ways than most programmers believe. But in many other ways it is different—in more ways than most professional managers expect.

The lore of the field is accumulating. There have been several conferences, sessions at AFIPS conferences, some books, and papers. But it is by no means yet in shape for any systematic textbook treatment. It seems appropriate, however, to offer this little book, reflecting essentially a personal view.

Although I originally grew up in the programming side of computer science, I was involved chiefly in hardware architecture during the years (1956–1963) that the autonomous control program and the high-level language compiler were developed. When in 1964 I became manager of Operating System/360, I found a programming world quite changed by the progress of the previous few years.

Managing OS/360 development was a very educational experience, albeit a very frustrating one. The team, including F. M. Trapnell who succeeded me as manager, has much to be proud of. The system contains many excellencies in design and execution, and it has been successful in achieving widespread use. Certain ideas, most noticeably device-independent input-output and external library management, were technical innovations now widely copied. It is now quite reliable, reasonably efficient, and very versatile.

The effort cannot be called wholly successful, however. Any OS/360 user is quickly aware of how much better it should be. The flaws in design and execution pervade especially the control program, as distinguished from the language compilers. Most of these flaws date from the 1964–65 design period and hence must be laid to my charge. Furthermore, the product was late, it took more memory than planned, the costs were several times the estimate, and it did not perform very well until several releases after the first.

After leaving IBM in 1965 to come to Chapel Hill as originally agreed when I took over OS/360, I began to analyze the OS/360 experience to see what management and technical lessons were to be learned. In particular, I wanted to explain the quite different management experiences encountered in System/360 hardware development and OS/360 software development. This book is a belated answer to Tom Watson's probing questions as to why programming is hard to manage.

In this quest I have profited from long conversations with R. P. Case, assistant manager 1964–65, and F. M. Trapnell, manager 1965–68. I have compared conclusions with other managers of jumbo programming projects, including F. J. Corbato of M.I.T., John Harr and V. Vyssotsky of Bell Telephone Laboratories, Charles Portman of International Computers Limited, A. P. Ershov of the Computation Laboratory of the Siberian Division, U.S.S.R. Academy of Sciences, and A. M. Pietrasanta of IBM.

My own conclusions are embodied in the essays that follow, which are intended for professional programmers, professional managers, and especially professional managers of programmers.

Although written as separable essays, there is a central argument contained especially in Chapters 2–7. Briefly, I believe that large programming projects suffer management problems different in kind from small ones, due to division of labor. I believe the critical need to be the preservation of the conceptual integrity of the product itself. These chapters explore both the difficulties of achieving this unity and methods for doing so. The later chapters explore other aspects of software engineering management.

The literature in this field is not abundant, but it is widely scattered. Hence I have tried to give references that will both illuminate particular points and guide the interested reader to other useful works. Many friends have read the manuscript, and some have prepared extensive helpful comments; where these seemed valuable but did not fit the flow of the text, I have included them in the notes.

Because this is a book of essays and not a text, all the references and notes have been banished to the end of the volume, and the reader is urged to ignore them on his first reading.

I am deeply indebted to Miss Sara Elizabeth Moore, Mr. David Wagner, and Mrs. Rebecca Burris for their help in preparing the manuscript, and to Professor Joseph C. Sloane for advice on illustration.

Chapel Hill, N.C.   F. P. B., Jr
October 1974

Contents

1
The Tar Pit

1
The Tar Pit

Een schip op het strand is een baken in zee.
[A ship on the beach is a lighthouse to the sea.]

DUTCH PROVERB

C. R. Knight, Mural of La Brea Tar Pits
The George C. Page Museum of La Brea Discoveries,
The Natural History Museum of Los Angeles County

No scene from prehistory is quite so vivid as that of the mortal struggles of great beasts in the tar pits. In the mind's eye one sees dinosaurs, mammoths, and sabertoothed tigers struggling against the grip of the tar. The fiercer the struggle, the more entangling the tar, and no beast is so strong or so skillful but that he ultimately sinks.

Large-system programming has over the past decade been such a tar pit, and many great and powerful beasts have thrashed violently in it. Most have emerged with running systems—few have met goals, schedules, and budgets. Large and small, massive or wiry, team after team has become entangled in the tar. No one thing seems to cause the difficulty—any particular paw can be pulled away. But the accumulation of simultaneous and interacting factors brings slower and slower motion. Everyone seems to have been surprised by the stickiness of the problem, and it is hard to discern the nature of it. But we must try to understand it if we are to solve it.

Therefore let us begin by identifying the craft of system programming and the joys and woes inherent in it.

The Programming Systems Product

One occasionally reads newspaper accounts of how two programmers in a remodeled garage have built an important program that surpasses the best efforts of large teams. And every programmer is prepared to believe such tales, for he knows that he could build *any* program much faster than the 1000 statements/year reported for industrial teams.

Why then have not all industrial programming teams been replaced by dedicated garage duos? One must look at *what* is being produced.

In the upper left of Fig. 1.1 is a *program*. It is complete in itself, ready to be run by the author on the system on which it was developed. *That* is the thing commonly produced in garages, and

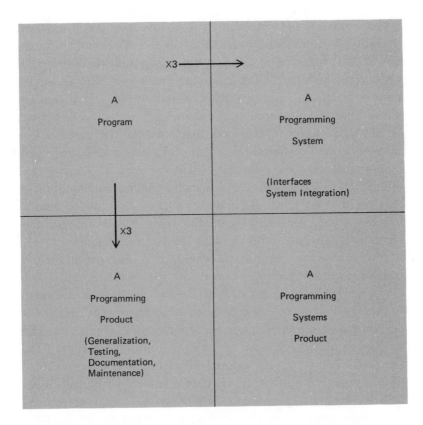

Fig. 1.1   Evolution of the programming systems product

that is the object the individual programmer uses in estimating productivity.

There are two ways a program can be converted into a more useful, but more costly, object. These two ways are represented by the boundaries in the diagram.

Moving down across the horizontal boundary, a program becomes a *programming product.* This is a program that can be run, tested, repaired, and extended by anybody. It is usable in many operating environments, for many sets of data. To become a generally usable programming product, a program must be written in a generalized fashion. In particular the range and form of inputs must be generalized as much as the basic algorithm will reasonably allow. Then the program must be thoroughly tested, so that it can be depended upon. This means that a substantial bank of test cases, exploring the input range and probing its boundaries, must be prepared, run, and recorded. Finally, promotion of a program to a programming product requires its thorough documentation, so that anyone may use it, fix it, and extend it. As a rule of thumb, I estimate that a programming product costs at least three times as much as a debugged program with the same function.

Moving across the vertical boundary, a program becomes a component in a *programming system.* This is a collection of interacting programs, coordinated in function and disciplined in format, so that the assemblage constitutes an entire facility for large tasks. To become a programming system component, a program must be written so that every input and output conforms in syntax and semantics with precisely defined interfaces. The program must also be designed so that it uses only a prescribed budget of resources—memory space, input-output devices, computer time. Finally, the program must be tested with other system components, in all expected combinations. This testing must be extensive, for the number of cases grows combinatorially. It is time-consuming, for subtle bugs arise from unexpected interactions of debugged components. A programming system component costs at least three times as much as a stand-alone program of the same function. The cost may be greater if the system has many components.

In the lower right-hand corner of Fig. 1.1 stands the *programming systems product.* This differs from the simple program in all of the above ways. It costs nine times as much. But it is the truly useful object, the intended product of most system programming efforts.

The Joys of the Craft

Why is programming fun? What delights may its practitioner expect as his reward?

First is the sheer joy of making things. As the child delights in his mud pie, so the adult enjoys building things, especially things of his own design. I think this delight must be an image of God's delight in making things, a delight shown in the distinctness and newness of each leaf and each snowflake.

Second is the pleasure of making things that are useful to other people. Deep within, we want others to use our work and to find it helpful. In this respect the programming system is not essentially different from the child's first clay pencil holder "for Daddy's office."

Third is the fascination of fashioning complex puzzle-like objects of interlocking moving parts and watching them work in subtle cycles, playing out the consequences of principles built in from the beginning. The programmed computer has all the fascination of the pinball machine or the jukebox mechanism, carried to the ultimate.

Fourth is the joy of always learning, which springs from the nonrepeating nature of the task. In one way or another the problem is ever new, and its solver learns something: sometimes practical, sometimes theoretical, and sometimes both.

Finally, there is the delight of working in such a tractable medium. The programmer, like the poet, works only slightly removed from pure thought-stuff. He builds his castles in the air, from air, creating by exertion of the imagination. Few media of creation are so flexible, so easy to polish and rework, so readily capable of realizing grand conceptual structures. (As we shall see later, this very tractability has its own problems.)

Yet the program construct, unlike the poet's words, is real in the sense that it moves and works, producing visible outputs separate from the construct itself. It prints results, draws pictures, produces sounds, moves arms. The magic of myth and legend has come true in our time. One types the correct incantation on a keyboard, and a display screen comes to life, showing things that never were nor could be.

Programming then is fun because it gratifies creative longings built deep within us and delights sensibilities we have in common with all men.

The Woes of the Craft

Not all is delight, however, and knowing the inherent woes makes it easier to bear them when they appear.

First, one must perform perfectly. The computer resembles the magic of legend in this respect, too. If one character, one pause, of the incantation is not strictly in proper form, the magic doesn't work. Human beings are not accustomed to being perfect, and few areas of human activity demand it. Adjusting to the requirement for perfection is, I think, the most difficult part of learning to program.[1]

Next, other people set one's objectives, provide one's resources, and furnish one's information. One rarely controls the circumstances of his work, or even its goal. In management terms, one's authority is not sufficient for his responsibility. It seems that in all fields, however, the jobs where things get done never have formal authority commensurate with responsibility. In practice, actual (as opposed to formal) authority is acquired from the very momentum of accomplishment.

The dependence upon others has a particular case that is especially painful for the system programmer. He depends upon other people's programs. These are often maldesigned, poorly implemented, incompletely delivered (no source code or test cases), and poorly documented. So he must spend hours studying and fixing things that in an ideal world would be complete, available, and usable.

The next woe is that designing grand concepts is fun; finding nitty little bugs is just work. With any creative activity come dreary hours of tedious, painstaking labor, and programming is no exception.

Next, one finds that debugging has a linear convergence, or worse, where one somehow expects a quadratic sort of approach to the end. So testing drags on and on, the last difficult bugs taking more time to find than the first.

The last woe, and sometimes the last straw, is that the product over which one has labored so long appears to be obsolete upon (or before) completion. Already colleagues and competitors are in hot pursuit of new and better ideas. Already the displacement of one's thought-child is not only conceived, but scheduled.

This always seems worse than it really is. The new and better product is generally not *available* when one completes his own; it is only talked about. It, too, will require months of development. The real tiger is never a match for the paper one, unless actual use is wanted. Then the virtues of reality have a satisfaction all their own.

Of course the technological base on which one builds is *always* advancing. As soon as one freezes a design, it becomes obsolete in terms of its concepts. But implementation of real products demands phasing and quantizing. The obsolescence of an implementation must be measured against other existing implementations, not against unrealized concepts. The challenge and the mission are to find real solutions to real problems on actual schedules with available resources.

This then is programming, both a tar pit in which many efforts have floundered and a creative activity with joys and woes all its own. For many, the joys far outweigh the woes, and for them the remainder of this book will attempt to lay some boardwalks across the tar.

2
The Mythical Man-Month

Restaurant Antoine

Fondé En 1840

ENTREES (SUITE)

Côtelettes d'agneau grillées 2.50
Côtelettes d'agneau aux champignons frais 2.75
Filet de boeuf aux champignons frais 4.75
Ris de veau à la financière 2.00
Filet de boeuf nature 3.75
Tournedos Médicis 3.25
Pigeonneaux sauce paradis 3.50
Tournedos sauce béarnaise 3.25
Entrecôte minute 2.75
Filet de boeuf béarnaise 4.00
Tripes à la mode de Caen (commander d'avance) 2.00

Entrecôte marchand de vin 4.00
Côtelettes d'agneau maison d'or 2.
Côtelettes d'agneau à la parisienne
Fois de volaille à la brochette 1.50
Tournedos nature 2.75
Filet de boeuf à la hawaïenne 4.00
Tournedos à la hawaïenne 3.25
Tournedos marchand de vin 3.25
Pigeonneaux grillés 3.00
Entrecôte nature 3.75
Châteaubriand (30 minutes)

LÉGUMES

Epinards sauce crème   .60   Chou-fleur au gratin   .60
Broccoli sauce hollandaise   .80   Asperges fraîches au beurre   .90
Pommes de terre au gratin   .60   Carottes à la crème   .60
Haricots verts au berre   .60   Pommes de terre soufflées
Petits pois à la française   .75

SALADES

Salade Antoine   .60
Salade Mirabeau   .75
Salade laitue au roquefort   .80
Salade de laitue aux tomates   .60
Salade de légumes   .60
Salade d'anchois 1.00

Fonds d'artichauts Bayard
Salade de laitue aux oeufs   .60
Tomate frappée à la Jules César   .60
Salade de coeur de palmier 1.00
Salade aux pointes d'asperges   .60
Avocat à la vinaigrette   .60

DESSERTS

Gâteau moka   .50
Méringue glacée   .60
Crêpes Suzette 1.25
Glace sauce chocolat   .60
Fruits de saison à l'eau-de-vie   .75
Omelette soufflée à la Jules César (2) 2.00
Omelette Alaska Antoine (2) 2.50

Cerises jubilé 1.25
Crêpes à la gelée   .80
Crêpes nature   .70
Omelette au rhum 1.10
Glace à la vanille   .5
Fraises au kirsch
Pêche Melba

FROMAGES

Roquefort   .50   Liederkranz   .50   Gruyère   .50
Camembert   .50   Fromage à la crême Philadelphie   .50

CAFÉ ET THÉ

Café   .20   Café au lait   .20   Thé   .20
Café brulôt diabolique 1.00   Thé glacé   .20   Demi-tasse

EAUX MINERALES—BIERE—CIGARES—CIGARETTES

White Rock   Bière locale   Cig
Vichy   Cliquot Club   Canada Dry   Cigarettes

Roy L. Alciatore, Propriétaire

713-717 Rue St. Louis   Nouvelle Orléans, Louisiane

2
The Mythical Man-Month

Good cooking takes time. If you are made to wait, it is to serve you better, and to please you.

MENU OF RESTAURANT ANTOINE, NEW ORLEANS

More software projects have gone awry for lack of calendar time than for all other causes combined. Why is this cause of disaster so common?

First, our techniques of estimating are poorly developed. More seriously, they reflect an unvoiced assumption which is quite untrue, i.e., that all will go well.

Second, our estimating techniques fallaciously confuse effort with progress, hiding the assumption that men and months are interchangeable.

Third, because we are uncertain of our estimates, software managers often lack the courteous stubbornness of Antoine's chef.

Fourth, schedule progress is poorly monitored. Techniques proven and routine in other engineering disciplines are considered radical innovations in software engineering.

Fifth, when schedule slippage is recognized, the natural (and traditional) response is to add manpower. Like dousing a fire with gasoline, this makes matters worse, much worse. More fire requires more gasoline, and thus begins a regenerative cycle which ends in disaster.

Schedule monitoring will be the subject of a separate essay. Let us consider other aspects of the problem in more detail.

Optimism

All programmers are optimists. Perhaps this modern sorcery especially attracts those who believe in happy endings and fairy godmothers. Perhaps the hundreds of nitty frustrations drive away all but those who habitually focus on the end goal. Perhaps it is merely that computers are young, programmers are younger, and the young are always optimists. But however the selection process works, the result is indisputable: "This time it will surely run," or "I just found the last bug."

So the first false assumption that underlies the scheduling of systems programming is that *all will go well,* i.e., that *each task will take only as long as it "ought" to take.*

The pervasiveness of optimism among programmers deserves more than a flip analysis. Dorothy Sayers, in her excellent book, *The Mind of the Maker,* divides creative activity into three stages: the idea, the implementation, and the interaction. A book, then, or a computer, or a program comes into existence first as an ideal construct, built outside time and space, but complete in the mind of the author. It is realized in time and space, by pen, ink, and paper, or by wire, silicon, and ferrite. The creation is complete when someone reads the book, uses the computer, or runs the program, thereby interacting with the mind of the maker.

This description, which Miss Sayers uses to illuminate not only human creative activity but also the Christian doctrine of the Trinity, will help us in our present task. For the human makers of things, the incompletenesses and inconsistencies of our ideas become clear only during implementation. Thus it is that writing, experimentation, "working out" are essential disciplines for the theoretician.

In many creative activities the medium of execution is intractable. Lumber splits; paints smear; electrical circuits ring. These physical limitations of the medium constrain the ideas that may be expressed, and they also create unexpected difficulties in the implementation.

Implementation, then, takes time and sweat both because of the physical media and because of the inadequacies of the underlying ideas. We tend to blame the physical media for most of our implementation difficulties; for the media are not "ours" in the way the ideas are, and our pride colors our judgment.

Computer programming, however, creates with an exceedingly tractable medium. The programmer builds from pure thought-stuff: concepts and very flexible representations thereof. Because the medium is tractable, we expect few difficulties in implementation; hence our pervasive optimism. Because our ideas are faulty, we have bugs; hence our optimism is unjustified.

In a single task, the assumption that all will go well has a probabilistic effect on the schedule. It might indeed go as planned, for there is a probability distribution for the delay that will be encountered, and "no delay" has a finite probability. A large programming effort, however, consists of many tasks, some chained end-to-end. The probability that each will go well becomes vanishingly small.

The Man-Month

The second fallacious thought mode is expressed in the very unit of effort used in estimating and scheduling: the man-month. Cost does indeed vary as the product of the number of men and the number of months. Progress does not. *Hence the man-month as a unit for measuring the size of a job is a dangerous and deceptive myth.* It implies that men and months are interchangeable.

Men and months are interchangeable commodities only when a task can be partitioned among many workers *with no communication among them* (Fig. 2.1). This is true of reaping wheat or picking cotton; it is not even approximately true of systems programming.

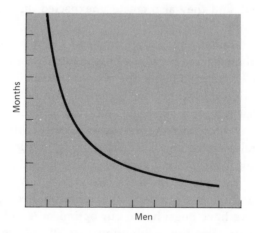

Fig. 2.1 Time versus number of workers—perfectly partitionable task

When a task cannot be partitioned because of sequential constraints, the application of more effort has no effect on the schedule (Fig. 2.2). The bearing of a child takes nine months, no matter
how many women are assigned. Many software tasks have this
characteristic because of the sequential nature of debugging.

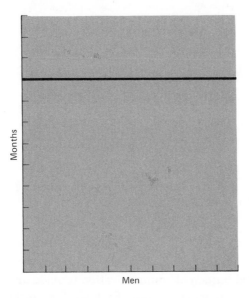

Fig. 2.2   Time versus number of workers—unpartitionable task

In tasks that can be partitioned but which require communication among the subtasks, the effort of communication must be
added to the amount of work to be done. Therefore the best that
can be done is somewhat poorer than an even trade of men for
months (Fig. 2.3).

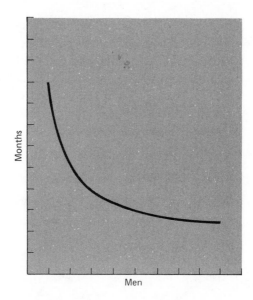

Fig. 2.3 Time versus number of workers—partitionable task requiring communication

The added burden of communication is made up of two parts, training and intercommunication. Each worker must be trained in the technology, the goals of the effort, the overall strategy, and the plan of work. This training cannot be partitioned, so this part of the added effort varies linearly with the number of workers.[1]

Intercommunication is worse. If each part of the task must be separately coordinated with each other part, the effort increases as $n(n-1)/2$. Three workers require three times as much pairwise intercommunication as two; four require six times as much as two. If, moreover, there need to be conferences among three, four, etc., workers to resolve things jointly, matters get worse yet. The added effort of communicating may fully counteract the division of the original task and bring us to the situation of Fig. 2.4.

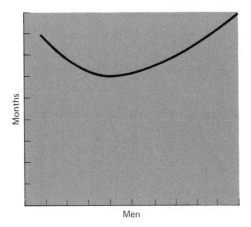

Fig. 2.4   Time versus number of workers—task with complex interrelationships

Since software construction is inherently a systems effort—an exercise in complex interrelationships—communication effort is great, and it quickly dominates the decrease in individual task time brought about by partitioning. Adding more men then lengthens, not shortens, the schedule.

Systems Test

No parts of the schedule are so thoroughly affected by sequential constraints as component debugging and system test. Furthermore, the time required depends on the number and subtlety of the errors encountered. Theoretically this number should be zero. Because of optimism, we usually expect the number of bugs to be smaller than it turns out to be. Therefore testing is usually the most mis-scheduled part of programming.

For some years I have been successfully using the following rule of thumb for scheduling a software task:

⅓ planning
⅙ coding
¼ component test and early system test
¼ system test, all components in hand.

This differs from conventional scheduling in several important ways:

1. The fraction devoted to planning is larger than normal. Even so, it is barely enough to produce a detailed and solid specification, and not enough to include research or exploration of totally new techniques.
2. The *half* of the schedule devoted to debugging of completed code is much larger than normal.
3. The part that is easy to estimate, i.e., coding, is given only one-sixth of the schedule.

In examining conventionally scheduled projects, I have found that few allowed one-half of the projected schedule for testing, but that most did indeed spend half of the actual schedule for that purpose. Many of these were on schedule until and except in system testing.[2]

Failure to allow enough time for system test, in particular, is peculiarly disastrous. Since the delay comes at the end of the schedule, no one is aware of schedule trouble until almost the delivery date. Bad news, late and without warning, is unsettling to customers and to managers.

Furthermore, delay at this point has unusually severe financial, as well as psychological, repercussions. The project is fully staffed, and cost-per-day is maximum. More seriously, the software is to support other business effort (shipping of computers, operation of new facilities, etc.) and the secondary costs of delaying these are very high, for it is almost time for software shipment.

Indeed, these secondary costs may far outweigh all others. It is therefore very important to allow enough system test time in the original schedule.

Gutless Estimating

Observe that for the programmer, as for the chef, the urgency of the patron may govern the scheduled completion of the task, but it cannot govern the actual completion. An omelette, promised in two minutes, may appear to be progressing nicely. But when it has not set in two minutes, the customer has two choices—wait or eat it raw. Software customers have had the same choices.

The cook has another choice; he can turn up the heat. The result is often an omelette nothing can save—burned in one part, raw in another.

Now I do not think software managers have less inherent courage and firmness than chefs, nor than other engineering managers. But false scheduling to match the patron's desired date is much more common in our discipline than elsewhere in engineering. It is very difficult to make a vigorous, plausible, and job-risking defense of an estimate that is derived by no quantitative method, supported by little data, and certified chiefly by the hunches of the managers.

Clearly two solutions are needed. We need to develop and publicize productivity figures, bug-incidence figures, estimating rules, and so on. The whole profession can only profit from sharing such data.

Until estimating is on a sounder basis, individual managers will need to stiffen their backbones and defend their estimates with the assurance that their poor hunches are better than wish-derived estimates.

Regenerative Schedule Disaster

What does one do when an essential software project is behind schedule? Add manpower, naturally. As Figs. 2.1 through 2.4 suggest, this may or may not help.

Let us consider an example.[3] Suppose a task is estimated at 12 man-months and assigned to three men for four months, and that there are measurable mileposts A, B, C, D, which are scheduled to fall at the end of each month (Fig. 2.5).

Now suppose the first milepost is not reached until two months have elapsed (Fig. 2.6). What are the alternatives facing the manager?

1. Assume that the task must be done on time. Assume that only the first part of the task was misestimated, so Fig. 2.6 tells the story accurately. Then 9 man-months of effort remain, and two months, so 4½ men will be needed. Add 2 men to the 3 assigned.

2. Assume that the task must be done on time. Assume that the whole estimate was uniformly low, so that Fig. 2.7 really describes the situation. Then 18 man-months of effort remain, and two months, so 9 men will be needed. Add 6 men to the 3 assigned.

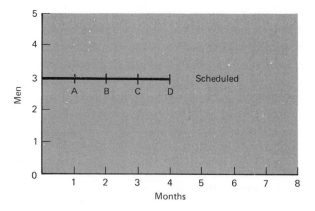

Figure 2.5

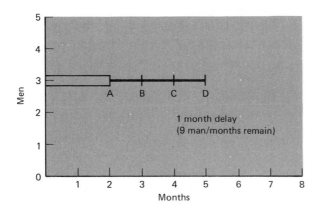

Figure 2.6

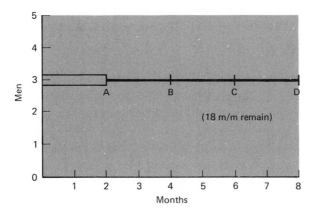

Figure 2.7

3. Reschedule. I like the advice given by P. Fagg, an experienced hardware engineer, "Take no small slips." That is, allow enough time in the new schedule to ensure that the work can be carefully and thoroughly done, and that rescheduling will not have to be done again.
4. Trim the task. In practice this tends to happen anyway, once the team observes schedule slippage. Where the secondary costs of delay are very high, this is the only feasible action. The manager's only alternatives are to trim it formally and carefully, to reschedule, or to watch the task get silently trimmed by hasty design and incomplete testing.

In the first two cases, insisting that the unaltered task be completed in four months is disastrous. Consider the regenerative effects, for example, for the first alternative (Fig. 2.8). The two new men, however competent and however quickly recruited, will require training in the task by one of the experienced men. If this takes a month, *3 man-months will have been devoted to work not in the original estimate.* Furthermore, the task, originally partitioned three ways, must be repartitioned into five parts; hence some work already done will be lost, and system testing must be lengthened. So at the end of the third month, substantially more than 7 man-months of effort remain, and 5 trained people and one month are available. As Fig. 2.8 suggests, the product is just as late as if no one had been added (Fig. 2.6).

To hope to get done in four months, considering only training time and not repartitioning and extra systems test, would require adding 4 men, not 2, at the end of the second month. To cover repartitioning and system test effects, one would have to add still other men. Now, however, one has at least a 7-man team, not a 3-man one; thus such aspects as team organization and task division are different in kind, not merely in degree.

Notice that by the end of the third month things look very black. The March 1 milestone has not been reached in spite of all

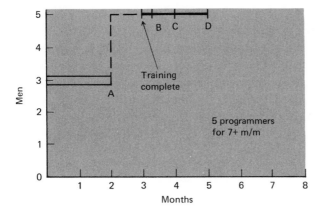

Figure 2.8

the managerial effort. The temptation is very strong to repeat the cycle, adding yet more manpower. Therein lies madness.

The foregoing assumed that only the first milestone was misestimated. If on March 1 one makes the conservative assumption that the whole schedule was optimistic, as Fig. 2.7 depicts, one wants to add 6 men just to the original task. Calculation of the training, repartitioning, system testing effects is left as an exercise for the reader. Without a doubt, the regenerative disaster will yield a poorer product, later, than would rescheduling with the original three men, unaugmented.

Oversimplifying outrageously, we state Brooks's Law:

Adding manpower to a late software project makes it later.

This then is the demythologizing of the man-month. The number of months of a project depends upon its sequential constraints. The maximum number of men depends upon the number of independent subtasks. From these two quantities one can derive schedules using fewer men and more months. (The only risk is product obsolescence.) One cannot, however, get workable schedules using more men and fewer months. More software projects have gone awry for lack of calendar time than for all other causes combined.

3
The Surgical Team

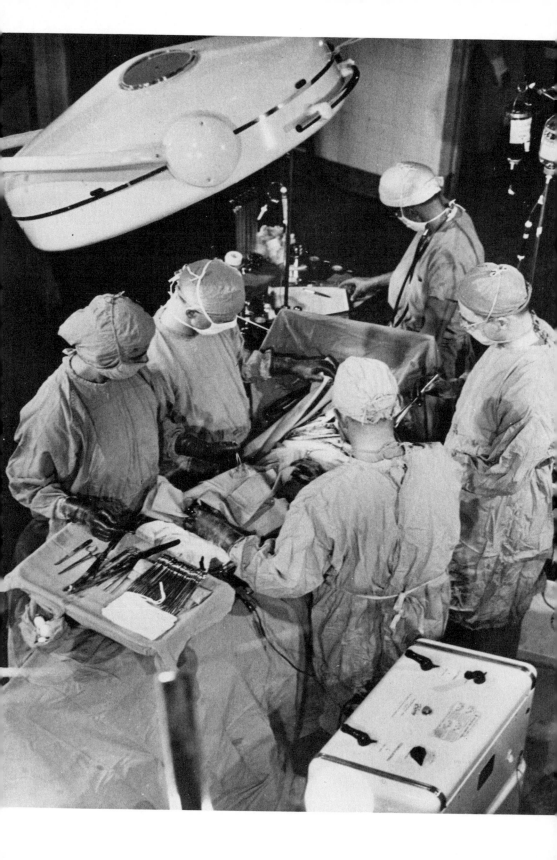

3
The Surgical Team

These studies revealed large individual differences between high and low performers, often by an order of magnitude.

SACKMAN, ERIKSON, AND GRANT[1]

At computer society meetings one continually hears young programming managers assert that they favor a small, sharp team of first-class people, rather than a project with hundreds of programmers, and those by implication mediocre. So do we all.

But this naive statement of the alternatives avoids the hard problem—how does one build *large* systems on a meaningful schedule? Let us look at each side of this question in more detail.

The Problem

Programming managers have long recognized wide productivity variations between good programmers and poor ones. But the actual measured magnitudes have astounded all of us. In one of their studies, Sackman, Erikson, and Grant were measuring performances of a group of experienced programmers. Within just this group the ratios between best and worst performances averaged about 10:1 on productivity measurements and an amazing 5:1 on program speed and space measurements! In short the $20,000/year programmer may well be 10 times as productive as the $10,000/year one. The converse may be true, too. The data showed no correlation whatsoever between experience and performance. (I doubt if that is universally true.)

I have earlier argued that the sheer number of minds to be coordinated affects the cost of the effort, for a major part of the cost is communication and correcting the ill effects of miscommunication (system debugging). This, too, suggests that one wants the system to be built by as few minds as possible. Indeed, most experience with large programming systems shows that the brute-force approach is costly, slow, inefficient, and produces systems that are not conceptually integrated. OS/360, Exec 8, Scope 6600, Multics, TSS, SAGE, etc.—the list goes on and on.

The conclusion is simple: if a 200-man project has 25 managers who are the most competent and experienced programmers, fire the 175 troops and put the managers back to programming.

Now let's examine this solution. On the one hand, it fails to approach the ideal of the *small* sharp team, which by common consensus shouldn't exceed 10 people. It is so large that it will need to have at least two levels of management, or about five managers. It will additionally need support in finance, personnel, space, secretaries, and machine operators.

On the other hand, the original 200-man team was not large enough to build the really large systems by brute-force methods. Consider OS/360, for example. At the peak over 1000 people were working on it—programmers, writers, machine operators, clerks, secretaries, managers, support groups, and so on. From 1963 through 1966 probably 5000 man-years went into its design, construction, and documentation. Our postulated 200-man team would have taken 25 years to have brought the product to its present stage, if men and months traded evenly!

This then is the problem with the small, sharp team concept: *it is too slow for really big systems.* Consider the OS/360 job as it might be tackled with a small, sharp team. Postulate a 10-man team. As a bound, let them be seven times as productive as mediocre programmers in both programming and documentation, because they are sharp. Assume OS/360 was built only by mediocre programmers (which is *far* from the truth). As a bound, assume that another productivity improvement factor of seven comes from reduced communication on the part of the smaller team. Assume the *same* team stays on the entire job. Well, 5000/(10 X 7 X 7) = 10; they can do the 5000 man-year job in 10 years. Will the product be interesting 10 years after its initial design? Or will it have been made obsolete by the rapidly developing software technology?

The dilemma is a cruel one. For efficiency and conceptual integrity, one prefers a few good minds doing design and construction. Yet for large systems one wants a way to bring considerable manpower to bear, so that the product can make a timely appearance. How can these two needs be reconciled?

Mills's Proposal

A proposal by Harlan Mills offers a fresh and creative solution.[2,3] Mills proposes that each segment of a large job be tackled by a team, but that the team be organized like a surgical team rather than a hog-butchering team. That is, instead of each member cutting away on the problem, one does the cutting and the others give him every support that will enhance his effectiveness and productivity.

A little thought shows that this concept meets the desiderata, if it can be made to work. Few minds are involved in design and construction, yet many hands are brought to bear. Can it work? Who are the anesthesiologists and nurses on a programming team, and how is the work divided? Let me freely mix metaphors to suggest how such a team might work if enlarged to include all conceivable support.

The surgeon.   Mills calls him a *chief programmer.* He personally defines the functional and performance specifications, designs the program, codes it, tests it, and writes its documentation. He writes in a structured programming language such as PL/I, and has effective access to a computing system which not only runs his tests but also stores the various versions of his programs, allows easy file updating, and provides text editing for his documentation. He needs great talent, ten years experience, and considerable systems and application knowledge, whether in applied mathematics, business data handling, or whatever.

The copilot.   He is the alter ego of the surgeon, able to do any part of the job, but is less experienced. His main function is to share in the design as a thinker, discussant, and evaluator. The surgeon tries ideas on him, but is not bound by his advice. The copilot often represents his team in discussions of function and interface with other teams. He knows all the code intimately. He researches alternative design strategies. He obviously serves as insurance against disaster to the surgeon. He may even write code, but he is not responsible for any part of the code.

The administrator.   The surgeon is boss, and he must have the last word on personnel, raises, space, and so on, but he must spend almost none of his time on these matters. Thus he needs a professional administrator who handles money, people, space, and machines, and who interfaces with the administrative machinery of the rest of the organization. Baker suggests that the administrator has a full-time job only if the project has substantial legal, contractual, reporting, or financial requirements because of the user-producer relationship. Otherwise, one administrator can serve two teams.

The editor.   The surgeon is responsible for generating the documentation—for maximum clarity he must write it. This is true of both external and internal descriptions. The editor, however, takes the draft or dictated manuscript produced by the surgeon and criticizes it, reworks it, provides it with references and bibliography, nurses it through several versions, and oversees the mechanics of production.

Two secretaries.   The administrator and the editor will each need a secretary; the administrator's secretary will handle project correspondence and non-product files.

The program clerk.   He is responsible for maintaining all the technical records of the team in a programming-product library. The clerk is trained as a secretary and has responsibility for both machine-readable and human-readable files.

All computer input goes to the clerk, who logs and keys it if required. The output listings go back to him to be filed and indexed. The most recent runs of any model are kept in a status notebook; all previous ones are filed in a chronological archive.

Absolutely vital to Mills's concept is the transformation of programming "from private art to public practice" by making *all* the computer runs visible to all team members and identifying all programs and data as team property, not private property.

The specialized function of the program clerk relieves programmers of clerical chores, systematizes and ensures proper performance of those oft-neglected chores, and enhances the team's most valuable asset—its work-product. Clearly the concept as set forth above assumes batch runs. When interactive terminals are used, particularly those with no hard-copy output, the program clerk's functions do not diminish, but they change. Now he logs all updates of team program copies from private working copies, still handles all batch runs, and uses his own interactive facility to control the integrity and availability of the growing product.

The toolsmith.   File-editing, text-editing, and interactive debugging services are now readily available, so that a team will rarely need its own machine and machine-operating crew. But these services must be available with unquestionably satisfactory response and reliability; and the surgeon must be sole judge of the adequacy of the service available to him. He needs a toolsmith, responsible for ensuring this adequacy of the basic service and for constructing, maintaining, and upgrading special tools—mostly interactive computer services—needed by his team. Each team will need its own toolsmith, regardless of the excellence and reliability of any centrally provided service, for his job is to see to the tools needed or wanted by *his* surgeon, without regard to any other team's needs. The tool-builder will often construct specialized utilities, catalogued procedures, macro libraries.

The tester.   The surgeon will need a bank of suitable test cases for testing pieces of his work as he writes it, and then for testing the whole thing. The tester is therefore both an adversary who devises system test cases from the functional specs, and an assistant who devises test data for the day-by-day debugging. He would also plan testing sequences and set up the scaffolding required for component tests.

The language lawyer.   By the time Algol came along, people began to recognize that most computer installations have one or two people who delight in mastery of the intricacies of a programming language. And these experts turn out to be very useful and very widely consulted. The talent here is rather different from that of the surgeon, who is primarily a system designer and who thinks representations. The language lawyer can find a neat and efficient way to use the language to do difficult, obscure, or tricky things. Often he will need to do small studies (two or three days) on good technique. One language lawyer can service two or three surgeons.

This, then, is how 10 people might contribute in well-differentiated and specialized roles on a programming team built on the surgical model.

How It Works

The team just defined meets the desiderata in several ways. Ten people, seven of them professionals, are at work on the problem, but the system is the product of one mind—or at most two, acting *uno animo.*

Notice in particular the differences between a team of two programmers conventionally organized and the surgeon-copilot team. First, in the conventional team the partners divide the work, and each is responsible for design and implementation of part of the work. In the surgical team, the surgeon and copilot are each cognizant of all of the design and all of the code. This saves the labor of allocating space, disk accesses, etc. It also ensures the conceptual integrity of the work.

Second, in the conventional team the partners are equal, and the inevitable differences of judgment must be talked out or compromised. Since the work and resources are divided, the differences in judgment are confined to overall strategy and interfacing, but they are compounded by differences of interest—e.g., whose space will be used for a buffer. In the surgical team, there are no differences of interest, and differences of judgment are settled by the surgeon unilaterally. These two differences—lack of division of the problem and the superior-subordinate relationship—make it possible for the surgical team to act *uno animo.*

Yet the specialization of function of the remainder of the team is the key to its efficiency, for it permits a radically simpler communication pattern among the members, as Fig. 3.1 shows.

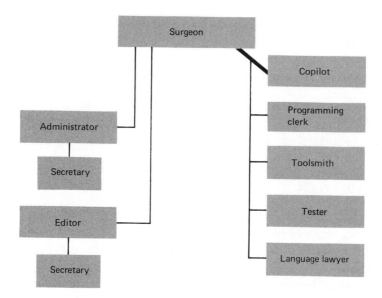

Fig. 3.1 Communication patterns in 10-man programming teams

Baker's article[3] reports on a single, small-scale test of the team concept. It worked as predicted for that case, with phenomenally good results.

Scaling Up

So far, so good. The problem, however, is how to build things that today take 5000 man-years, not things that take 20 or 30. A 10-man team can be effective no matter how it is organized, if the *whole* job is within its purview. But how is the surgical team concept to be used on large jobs when several hundred people are brought to bear on the task?

The success of the scaling-up process depends upon the fact that the conceptual integrity of each piece has been radically improved—that the number of minds determining the design has been divided by seven. So it is possible to put 200 people on a problem and face the problem of coordinating only 20 minds, those of the surgeons.

For that coordination problem, however, separate techniques must be used, and these are discussed in succeeding chapters. Let it suffice here to say that the entire system also must have conceptual integrity, and that requires a system architect to design it all, from the top down. To make that job manageable, a sharp distinction must be made between architecture and implementation, and the system architect must confine himself scrupulously to architecture. However, such roles and techniques have been shown to be feasible and, indeed, very productive.

4
Aristocracy, Democracy, and System Design

4
Aristocracy, Democracy, and System Design

This great church is an incomparable work of art. There is neither aridity nor confusion in the tenets it sets forth. . . .

It is the zenith of a style, the work of artists who had understood and assimilated all their predecessors' successes, in complete possession of the techniques of their times, but using them without indiscreet display nor gratuitous feats of skill.

It was Jean d'Orbais who undoubtedly conceived the general plan of the building, a plan which was respected, at least in its essential elements, by his successors. This is one of the reasons for the extreme coherence and unity of the edifice.

REIMS CATHEDRAL GUIDEBOOK[1]

Photographies Emmanuel Boudot-Lamotte

41

Conceptual Integrity

Most European cathedrals show differences in plan or architectural style between parts built in different generations by different builders. The later builders were tempted to "improve" upon the designs of the earlier ones, to reflect both changes in fashion and differences in individual taste. So the peaceful Norman transept abuts and contradicts the soaring Gothic nave, and the result proclaims the pridefulness of the builders as much as the glory of God.

Against these, the architectural unity of Reims stands in glorious contrast. The joy that stirs the beholder comes as much from the integrity of the design as from any particular excellences. As the guidebook tells, this integrity was achieved by the self-abnegation of eight generations of builders, each of whom sacrificed some of his ideas so that the whole might be of pure design. The result proclaims not only the glory of God, but also His power to salvage fallen men from their pride.

Even though they have not taken centuries to build, most programming systems reflect conceptual disunity far worse than that of cathedrals. Usually this arises not from a serial succession of master designers, but from the separation of design into many tasks done by many men.

I will contend that conceptual integrity is *the* most important consideration in system design. It is better to have a system omit certain anomalous features and improvements, but to reflect one set of design ideas, than to have one that contains many good but independent and uncoordinated ideas. In this chapter and the next two, we will examine the consequences of this theme for programming system design:

- How is conceptual integrity to be achieved?
- Does not this argument imply an elite, or aristocracy of architects, and a horde of plebeian implementers whose creative talents and ideas are suppressed?

- How does one keep the architects from drifting off into the blue with unimplementable or costly specifications?
- How does one ensure that every trifling detail of an architectural specification gets communicated to the implementer, properly understood by him, and accurately incorporated into the product?

Achieving Conceptual Integrity

The purpose of a programming system is to make a computer easy to use. To do this, it furnishes languages and various facilities that are in fact programs invoked and controlled by language features. But these facilities are bought at a price: the external description of a programming system is ten to twenty times as large as the external description of the computer system itself. The user finds it far easier to specify any particular function, but there are far more to choose from, and far more options and formats to remember.

Ease of use is enhanced only if the time gained in functional specification exceeds the time lost in learning, remembering, and searching manuals. With modern programming systems this gain does exceed the cost, but in recent years the ratio of gain to cost seems to have fallen as more and more complex functions have been added. I am haunted by the memory of the ease of use of the IBM 650, even without an assembler or any other software at all.

Because ease of use is the purpose, this ratio of function to conceptual complexity is the ultimate test of system design. Neither function alone nor simplicity alone defines a good design.

This point is widely misunderstood. Operating System/360 is hailed by its builders as the finest ever built, because it indisputably has the most function. Function, and not simplicity, has always been the measure of excellence for its designers. On the other hand, the Time-Sharing System for the PDP-10 is hailed by its builders as the finest, because of its simplicity and the spareness of its concepts. By any measure, however, its function is not even in the same class as that of OS/360. As soon as ease of use is held up as the criterion, each of these is seen to be unbalanced, reaching for only half of the true goal.

For a given level of function, however, that system is best in which one can specify things with the most simplicity and straightforwardness. *Simplicity* is not enough. Mooers's TRAC language and Algol 68 achieve simplicity as measured by the number of distinct elementary concepts. They are not, however, *straightforward.* The expression of the things one wants to do often requires involuted and unexpected combinations of the basic facilities. It is not enough to learn the elements and rules of combination; one must also learn the idiomatic usage, a whole lore of how the elements are combined in practice. Simplicity and straightforwardness proceed from conceptual integrity. Every part must reflect the same philosophies and the same balancing of desiderata. Every part must even use the same techniques in syntax and analogous notions in semantics. Ease of use, then, dictates unity of design, conceptual integrity.

Aristocracy and Democracy

Conceptual integrity in turn dictates that the design must proceed from one mind, or from a very small number of agreeing resonant minds.

Schedule pressures, however, dictate that system building needs many hands. Two techniques are available for resolving this dilemma. The first is a careful division of labor between architecture and implementation. The second is the new way of structuring programming implementation teams discussed in the previous chapter.

The separation of architectural effort from implementation is a very powerful way of getting conceptual integrity on very large projects. I myself have seen it used with great success on IBM's Stretch computer and on the System/360 computer product line.

I have seen it fail through lack of application on Operating System/360.

By the *architecture* of a system, I mean the complete and detailed specification of the user interface. For a computer this is the programming manual. For a compiler it is the language manual. For a control program it is the manuals for the language or languages used to invoke its functions. For the entire system it is the union of the manuals the user must consult to do his entire job.

The architect of a system, like the architect of a building, is the user's agent. It is his job to bring professional and technical knowledge to bear in the unalloyed interest of the user, as opposed to the interests of the salesman, the fabricator, etc.[2]

Architecture must be carefully distinguished from implementation. As Blaauw has said, "Where architecture tells *what* happens, implementation tells *how* it is made to happen."[3] He gives as a simple example a clock, whose architecture consists of the face, the hands, and the winding knob. When a child has learned this architecture, he can tell time as easily from a wristwatch as from a church tower. The implementation, however, and its realization, describe what goes on inside the case—powering by any of many mechanisms and accuracy control by any of many.

In System/360, for example, a single computer architecture is implemented quite differently in each of some nine models. Conversely, a single implementation, the Model 30 data flow, memory, and microcode, serves at different times for four different architectures: a System/360 computer, a multiplex channel with up to 224 logically independent subchannels, a selector channel, and a 1401 computer.[4]

The same distinction is equally applicable to programming systems. There is a U.S. standard Fortran IV. This is the architecture for many compilers. Within this architecture many implementations are possible: text-in-core or compiler-in-core, fast-compile or optimizing, syntax-directed or *ad-hoc*. Likewise any assembler language or job-control language admits of many implementations of the assembler or scheduler.

Now we can deal with the deeply emotional question of aristocracy versus democracy. Are not the architects a new aristocracy, an intellectual elite, set up to tell the poor dumb implementers what to do? Has not all the creative work been sequestered for this elite, leaving the implementers as cogs in the machine? Won't one get a better product by getting the good ideas from all the team, following a democratic philosophy, rather than by restricting the development of specifications to a few?

As to the last question, it is the easiest. I will certainly not contend that only the architects will have good architectural ideas. Often the fresh concept does come from an implementer or from a user. However, all my own experience convinces me, and I have tried to show, that the conceptual integrity of a system determines its ease of use. Good features and ideas that do not integrate with a system's basic concepts are best left out. If there appear many such important but incompatible ideas, one scraps the whole system and starts again on an integrated system with different basic concepts.

As to the aristocracy charge, the answer must be yes and no. Yes, in the sense that there must be few architects, their product must endure longer than that of an implementer, and the architect sits at the focus of forces which he must ultimately resolve in the user's interest. If a system is to have conceptual integrity, someone must control the concepts. That is an aristocracy that needs no apology.

No, because the setting of external specifications is not more creative work than the designing of implementations. It is just different creative work. The design of an implementation, given an architecture, requires and allows as much design creativity, as many new ideas, and as much technical brilliance as the design of the external specifications. Indeed, the cost-performance ratio of the product will depend most heavily on the implementer, just as ease of use depends most heavily on the architect.

There are many examples from other arts and crafts that lead one to believe that discipline is good for art. Indeed, an artist's aphorism asserts, "Form is liberating." The worst buildings are those whose budget was too great for the purposes to be served. Bach's creative output hardly seems to have been squelched by the necessity of producing a limited-form cantata each week. I am sure that the Stretch computer would have had a better architecture had it been more tightly constrained; the constraints imposed by the System/360 Model 30's budget were in my opinion entirely beneficial for the Model 75's architecture.

Similarly, I observe that the external provision of an architecture enhances, not cramps, the creative style of an implementing group. They focus at once on the part of the problem no one has addressed, and inventions begin to flow. In an unconstrained implementing group, most thought and debate goes into architectural decisions, and implementation proper gets short shrift.[5]

This effect, which I have seen many times, is confirmed by R. W. Conway, whose group at Cornell built the PL/C compiler for the PL/I language. He says, "We finally decided to implement the language unchanged and unimproved, for the debates about language would have taken all our effort."[6]

What Does the Implementer Do While Waiting?

It is a very humbling experience to make a multimillion-dollar mistake, but it is also very memorable. I vividly recall the night we decided how to organize the actual writing of external specifications for OS/360. The manager of architecture, the manager of control program implementation, and I were threshing out the plan, schedule, and division of responsibilities.

The architecture manager had 10 good men. He asserted that they could write the specifications and do it right. It would take ten months, three more than the schedule allowed.

The control program manager had 150 men. He asserted that they could prepare the specifications, with the architecture team coordinating; it would be well-done and practical, and he could do it on schedule. Furthermore, if the architecture team did it, his 150 men would sit twiddling their thumbs for ten months.

To this the architecture manager responded that if I gave the control program team the responsibility, the result would *not* in fact be on time, but would also be three months late, and of much lower quality. I did, and it was. He was right on both counts. Moreover, the lack of conceptual integrity made the system far more costly to build and change, and I would estimate that it added a year to debugging time.

Many factors, of course, entered into that mistaken decision; but the overwhelming one was schedule time and the appeal of putting all those 150 implementers to work. It is this siren song whose deadly hazards I would now make visible.

When it is proposed that a small architecture team in fact write all the external specifications for a computer or a programming system, the implementers raise three objections:

- The specifications will be too rich in function and will not reflect practical cost considerations.
- The architects will get all the creative fun and shut out the inventiveness of the implementers.
- The many implementers will have to sit idly by while the specifications come through the narrow funnel that is the architecture team.

The first of these is a real danger, and it will be treated in the next chapter. The other two are illusions, pure and simple. As we have seen above, implementation is also a creative activity of the first order. The opportunity to be creative and inventive in implementation is not significantly diminished by working within a given external specification, and the order of creativity may even be enhanced by that discipline. The total product will surely be.

The last objection is one of timing and phasing. A quick answer is to refrain from hiring implementers until the specifications are complete. This is what is done when a building is constructed.

In the computer systems business, however, the pace is quicker, and one wants to compress the schedule as much as possible. How much can specification and building be overlapped?

As Blaauw points out, the total creative effort involves three distinct phases: architecture, implementation, and realization. It turns out that these can in fact be begun in parallel and proceed simultaneously.

In computer design, for example, the implementer can start as soon as he has relatively vague assumptions about the manual, somewhat clearer ideas about the technology, and well-defined cost and performance objectives. He can begin designing data flows, control sequences, gross packaging concepts, and so on. He devises or adapts the tools he will need, especially the record-keeping system, including the design automation system.

Meanwhile, at the realization level, circuits, cards, cables, frames, power supplies, and memories must each be designed, refined, and documented. This work proceeds in parallel with architecture and implementation.

The same thing is true in programming system design. Long before the external specifications are complete, the implementer has plenty to do. Given some rough approximations as to the function of the system that will be ultimately embodied in the external specifications, he can proceed. He must have well-defined space and time objectives. He must know the system configuration on which his product must run. Then he can begin designing module boundaries, table structures, pass or phase breakdowns, algorithms, and all kinds of tools. Some time, too, must be spent in communicating with the architect.

Meanwhile, on the realization level there is much to be done also. Programming has a technology, too. If the machine is a new one, much work must be done on subroutine conventions, supervisory techniques, searching and sorting algorithms.[7]

Conceptual integrity does require that a system reflect a single philosophy and that the specification as seen by the user flow from a few minds. Because of the real division of labor into architecture, implementation, and realization, however, this does not imply that a system so designed will take longer to build. Experience shows the opposite, that the integral system goes together faster and takes less time to test. In effect, a widespread horizontal division of labor has been sharply reduced by a vertical division of labor, and the result is radically simplified communications and improved conceptual integrity.

5
The Second-System Effect

5
The Second-System Effect

Adde parvum parvo magnus acervus erit.
[Add little to little and there will be a big pile.]

OVID

Turning house for air traffic. Lithograph, Paris, 1882
From *Le Vingtième Siècle* by A. Robida

If one separates responsibility for functional specification from responsibility for building a fast, cheap product, what discipline bounds the architect's inventive enthusiasm?

The fundamental answer is thoroughgoing, careful, and sympathetic communication between architect and builder. Nevertheless there are finer-grained answers that deserve attention.

Interactive Discipline for the Architect

The architect of a building works against a budget, using estimating techniques that are later confirmed or corrected by the contractors' bids. It often happens that all the bids exceed the budget. The architect then revises his estimating technique upward and his design downward for another iteration. He may perhaps suggest to the contractors ways to implement his design more cheaply than they had devised.

An analogous process governs the architect of a computer system or a programming system. He has, however, the advantage of getting bids from the contractor at many early points in his design, almost any time he asks for them. He usually has the disadvantage of working with only one contractor, who can raise or lower his estimates to reflect his pleasure with the design. In practice, early and continuous communication can give the architect good cost readings and the builder confidence in the design without blurring the clear division of responsibilities.

The architect has two possible answers when confronted with an estimate that is too high: cut the design or challenge the estimate by suggesting cheaper implementations. This latter is inherently an emotion-generating activity. The architect is now challenging the builder's way of doing the builder's job. For it to be successful, the architect must

- remember that the builder has the inventive and creative responsibility for the implementation; so the architect suggests, not dictates;

- always be prepared to suggest *a* way of implementing any-thing he specifies, and be prepared to accept any other way that meets the objectives as well;
- deal quietly and privately in such suggestions;
- be ready to forego credit for suggested improvements.

Normally the builder will counter by suggesting changes to the architecture. Often he is right—some minor feature may have unexpectedly large costs when the implementation is worked out.

Self-Discipline—The Second-System Effect

An architect's first work is apt to be spare and clean. He knows he doesn't know what he's doing, so he does it carefully and with great restraint.

As he designs the first work, frill after frill and embellishment after embellishment occur to him. These get stored away to be used "next time." Sooner or later the first system is finished, and the architect, with firm confidence and a demonstrated mastery of that class of systems, is ready to build a second system.

This second is the most dangerous system a man ever designs. When he does his third and later ones, his prior experiences will confirm each other as to the general characteristics of such systems, and their differences will identify those parts of his experience that are particular and not generalizable.

The general tendency is to over-design the second system, using all the ideas and frills that were cautiously sidetracked on the first one. The result, as Ovid says, is a "big pile." For example, consider the IBM 709 architecture, later embodied in the 7090. This is an upgrade, a second system for the very successful and clean 704. The operation set is so rich and profuse that only about half of it was regularly used.

Consider as a stronger case the architecture, implementation, and even the realization of the Stretch computer, an outlet for the pent-up inventive desires of many people, and a second system for most of them. As Strachey says in a review:

> *I get the impression that Stretch is in some way the end of one line of development. Like some early computer programs it is immensely ingenious, immensely complicated, and extremely effective, but somehow at the same time crude, wasteful, and inelegant, and one feels that there must be a better way of doing things.* [1]

Operating System/360 was the second system for most of its designers. Groups of its designers came from building the 1410-7010 disk operating system, the Stretch operating system, the Project Mercury real-time system, and IBSYS for the 7090. Hardly anyone had experience with *two* previous operating systems.[2] So OS/360 is a prime example of the second-system effect, a Stretch of the software art to which both the commendations and the reproaches of Strachey's critique apply unchanged.

For example, OS/360 devotes 26 bytes of the permanently resident date-turnover routine to the proper handling of December 31 on leap years (when it is Day 366). That might have been left to the operator.

The second-system effect has another manifestation somewhat different from pure functional embellishment. That is a tendency to refine techniques whose very existence has been made obsolete by changes in basic system assumptions. OS/360 has many examples of this.

Consider the linkage editor, designed to load separately-compiled programs and resolve their cross-references. Beyond this basic function it also handles program overlays. It is one of the finest overlay facilities ever built. It allows overlay structuring to be done externally, at linkage time, without being designed into the source code. It allows the overlay structure to be changed from run to run without recompilation. It furnishes a rich variety of useful options and facilities. In a sense it is the culmination of years of development of static overlay technique.

Yet it is also the last and finest of the dinosaurs, for it belongs to a system in which multiprogramming is the normal mode and dynamic core allocation the basic assumption. This is in direct conflict with the notion of using static overlays. How much better the system would work if the efforts devoted to overlay management had been spent on making the dynamic core allocation and the dynamic cross-referencing facilities really fast!

Furthermore, the linkage editor requires so much space and itself contains many overlays that even when it is used just for linkage without overlay management, it is slower than most of the system compilers. The irony of this is that the purpose of the linker is to avoid recompilation. Like a skater whose stomach gets ahead of his feet, refinement proceeded until the system assumptions had been quite outrun.

The TESTRAN debugging facility is another example of this tendency. It is the culmination of batch debugging facilities, furnishing truly elegant snapshot and core dump capabilities. It uses the control section concept and an ingenious generator technique to allow selective tracing and snapshotting without interpretive overhead or recompilation. The imaginative concepts of the Share Operating System[3] for the 709 have been brought to full bloom.

Meanwhile, the whole notion of batch debugging without recompilation was becoming obsolete. Interactive computing systems, using language interpreters or incremental compilers have provided the most fundamental challenge. But even in batch systems, the appearance of fast-compile/slow-execute compilers has made source-level debugging and snapshotting the preferred technique. How much better the system would have been if the TESTRAN effort had been devoted instead to building the interactive and fast-compile facilities earlier and better!

Yet another example is the scheduler, which provides truly excellent facilities for managing a fixed-batch job stream. In a real sense, this scheduler is the refined, improved, and embellished second system succeeding the 1410-7010 Disk Operating System, a batch system unmultiprogrammed except for input-output and intended chiefly for business applications. As such, the OS/360 scheduler is good. But it is almost totally uninfluenced by the OS/360 needs of remote job entry, multiprogramming, and permanently resident interactive subsystems. Indeed, the scheduler's design makes these hard.

How does the architect avoid the second-system effect? Well, obviously he can't skip his second system. But he can be conscious of the peculiar hazards of that system, and exert extra self-discipline to avoid functional ornamentation and to avoid extrapolation of functions that are obviated by changes in assumptions and purposes.

A discipline that will open an architect's eyes is to assign each little function a value: capability x is worth not more than m bytes of memory and n microseconds per invocation. These values will guide initial decisions and serve during implementation as a guide and warning to all.

How does the project manager avoid the second-system effect? By insisting on a senior architect who has at least two systems under his belt. Too, by staying aware of the special temptations, he can ask the right questions to ensure that the philosophical concepts and objectives are fully reflected in the detailed design.

6
Passing the Word

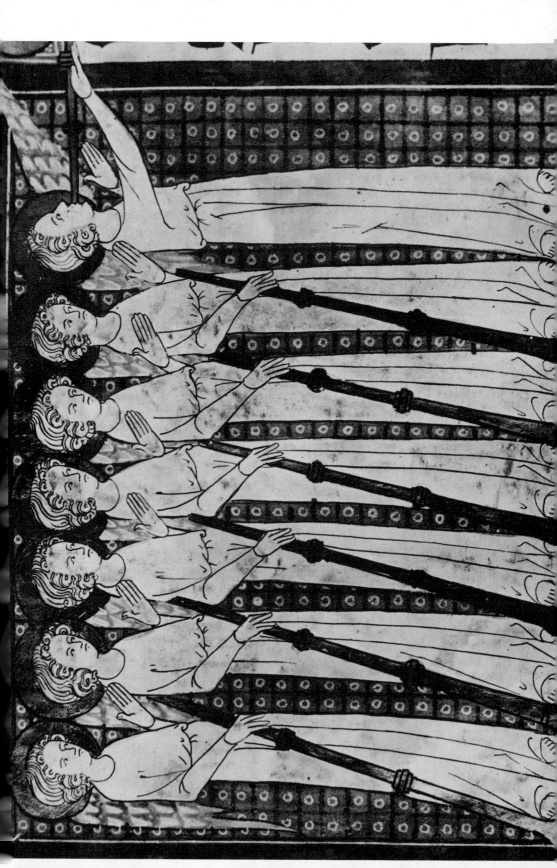

6
Passing the Word

He'll sit here and he'll say, "Do this! Do that!" And nothing will happen.

HARRY S. TRUMAN, ON PRESIDENTIAL POWER [1]

"The Seven Trumpets" from *The Wells Apocalypse,* 14th century
The Bettman Archive

Assuming that he has the disciplined, experienced architects and that there are many implementers, how shall the manager ensure that everyone hears, understands, and implements the architects' decisions? How can a group of 10 architects maintain the conceptual integrity of a system which 1000 men are building? A whole technology for doing this was worked out for the System/360 hardware design effort, and it is equally applicable to software projects.

Written Specifications—the Manual

The manual, or written specification, is a necessary tool, though not a sufficient one. The manual is the *external* specification of the product. It describes and prescribes every detail of what the user sees. As such, it is the chief product of the architect.

Round and round goes its preparation cycle, as feedback from users and implementers shows where the design is awkward to use or build. For the sake of implementers it is important that the changes be quantized—that there be dated versions appearing on a schedule.

The manual must not only describe everything the user does see, including all interfaces; it must also refrain from describing what the user does not see. That is the implementer's business, and there his design freedom must be unconstrained. The architect must always be prepared to show *an* implementation for any feature he describes, but he must not attempt to dictate *the* implementation.

The style must be precise, full, and accurately detailed. A user will often refer to a single definition, so each one must repeat all the essentials and yet all must agree. This tends to make manuals dull reading, but precision is more important than liveliness.

The unity of System/360's *Principles of Operation* springs from the fact that only two pens wrote it: Gerry Blaauw's and Andris Padegs'. The ideas are those of about ten men, but the casting of those decisions into prose specifications must be done by only one or two, if the consistency of prose and product is to be maintained. For the writing of a definition will necessitate a host of mini-decisions which are not of full-debate importance. An example in System/360 is the detail of how the Condition Code is set after each operation. *Not* trivial, however, is the principle that such mini-decisions be made consistently throughout.

I think the finest piece of manual writing I have ever seen is Blaauw's Appendix to *System/360 Principles of Operation*. This describes with care and precision the *limits* of System/360 compatibility. It defines compatibility, prescribes what is to be achieved, and enumerates those areas of external appearance where the architecture is intentionally silent and where results from one model may differ from those of another, where one copy of a given model may differ from another copy, or where a copy may differ even from itself after an engineering change. This is the level of precision to which manual writers aspire, and they must define what is *not* prescribed as carefully as what is.

Formal Definitions

English, or any other human language, is not naturally a precision instrument for such definitions. Therefore the manual writer must strain himself and his language to achieve the precision needed. An attractive alternative is to use a formal notation for such definitions. After all, precision is the stock in trade, the *raison d'être* of formal notations.

Let us examine the merits and weaknesses of formal definitions. As noted, formal definitions are precise. They tend to be complete; gaps show more conspicuously, so they are filled sooner. What they lack is comprehensibility. With English prose one can show structural principles, delineate structure in stages or levels, and give examples. One can readily mark exceptions and emphasize contrasts. Most important, one can explain *why*. The formal definitions put forward so far have inspired wonder at their elegance and confidence in their precision. But they have demanded prose explanations to make their content easy to learn and teach. For these reasons, I think we will see future specifications to consist of both a formal definition *and* a prose definition.

An ancient adage warns, "Never go to sea with two chronometers; take one or three." The same thing clearly applies to prose and formal definitions. If one has both, one must be the standard, and the other must be a derivative description, clearly labeled as such. Either can be the primary standard. Algol 68 has a formal definition as standard and a prose definition as descriptive. PL/I has the prose as standard and the formal description as derivative. System/360 also has prose as standard with a derived formal description.

Many tools are available for formal definition. The Backus-Naur Form is familiar for language definition, and it is amply discussed in the literature.[2] The formal description of PL/I uses new notions of abstract syntax, and it is adequately described.[3] Iverson's APL has been used to describe machines, most notably the IBM 7090[4] and System/360.[5]

Bell and Newell have proposed new notations for describing both configurations and machine architectures, and they have illustrated these with several machines, including the DEC PDP-8,[3] the 7090,[6] and System/360.[7]

Almost all formal definitions turn out to embody or describe an implementation of the hardware or software system whose externals they are prescribing. Syntax can be described without this, but semantics are usually defined by giving a program that carries out the defined operation. This is of course an implementation, and as such it over-prescribes the architecture. So one must take care to indicate that the formal definition applies only to externals, and one must say what these are.

Not only is a formal definition an implementation, an implementation can serve as a formal definition. When the first compatible computers were built, this was exactly the technique used. The new machine was to match an existing machine. The manual was vague on some points? "Ask the machine!" A test program would be devised to determine the behavior, and the new machine would be built to match.

A programmed simulator of a hardware or software system can serve in precisely the same way. It is an implementation; it runs. So all questions of definition can be resolved by testing it.

Using an implementation as a definition has some advantages. All questions can be settled unambiguously by experiment. Debate is never needed, so answers are quick. Answers are always as precise as one wants, and they are always correct, by definition. Opposed to these one has a formidable set of disadvantages. The implementation may over-prescribe even the externals. Invalid syntax always produces some result; in a policed system that result is an invalidity indication *and nothing more.* In an unpoliced system all kinds of side effects may appear, and these may have been used by programmers. When we undertook to emulate the IBM 1401 on System/360, for example, it developed that there were 30 different "curios"—side effects of supposedly invalid operations— that had come into widespread use and had to be considered as part of the definition. The implementation as a definition overprescribed; it not only said what the machine must do, it also said a great deal about how it had to do it.

Then, too, the implementation will sometimes give unexpected and unplanned answers when sharp questions are asked, and the *de facto* definition will often be found to be inelegant in these particulars precisely because they have never received any thought. This inelegance will often turn out to be slow or costly to duplicate in another implementation. For example, some machines leave trash in the multiplicand register after a multiplication. The precise nature of this trash turns out to be part of the *de facto* definition, yet duplicating it may preclude the use of a faster multiplication algorithm.

Finally, the use of an implementation as a formal definition is peculiarly susceptible to confusion as to whether the prose description or the formal description is in fact the standard. This is especially true of programmed simulations. One must also refrain from modifications to the implementation while it is serving as a standard.

Direct Incorporation

A lovely technique for disseminating and enforcing definitions is available for the software system architect. It is especially useful for establishing the syntax, if not the semantics, of intermodule interfaces. This technique is to design the declaration of the passed parameters or shared storage, and to require the implementations to include that declaration via a compile-time operation (a macro or a %INCLUDE in PL/I). If, in addition, the whole interface is referenced only by symbolic names, the declaration can be changed by adding or inserting new variables with only recompilation, not alteration, of the using program.

Conferences and Courts

Needless to say, meetings are necessary. The hundreds of man-to-man consultations must be supplemented by larger and more formal gatherings. We found two levels of these to be useful. The first is a weekly half-day conference of all the architects, plus official representatives of the hardware and software implementers, and the market planners. The chief system architect presides.

Anyone can propose problems or changes, but proposals are usually distributed in writing before the meeting. A new problem is usually discussed a while. The emphasis is on creativity, rather than merely decision. The group attempts to invent many solutions to problems, then a few solutions are passed to one or more of the architects for detailing into precisely worded manual change proposals.

Detailed change proposals then come up for decisions. These have been circulated and carefully considered by implementers and users, and the pros and cons are well delineated. If a consensus emerges, well and good. If not, the chief architect decides. Minutes are kept and decisions are formally, promptly, and widely disseminated.

Decisions from the weekly conferences give quick results and allow work to proceed. If anyone is *too* unhappy, instant appeals to the project manager are possible, but this happens very rarely.

The fruitfulness of these meetings springs from several sources:

1. The same group—architects, users, and implementers—meets weekly for months. No time is needed for bringing people up to date.
2. The group is bright, resourceful, well versed in the issues, and deeply involved in the outcome. No one has an "advisory" role. Everyone is authorized to make binding commitments.
3. When problems are raised, solutions are sought both within and outside the obvious boundaries.
4. The formality of written proposals focuses attention, forces decision, and avoids committee-drafted inconsistencies.
5. The clear vesting of decision-making power in the chief architect avoids compromise and delay.

As time goes by, some decisions don't wear well. Some minor matters have never been wholeheartedly accepted by one or another of the participants. Other decisions have developed unforeseen problems, and sometimes the weekly meeting didn't agree to reconsider these. So there builds up a backlog of minor appeals, open issues, or disgruntlements. To settle these we held annual supreme court sessions, lasting typically two weeks. (I would hold them every six months if I were doing it again.)

These sessions were held just before major freeze dates for the manual. Those present included not only the architecture group and the programmers' and implementers' architectural representatives, but also the managers of programming, marketing, and implementation efforts. The System/360 project manager presided. The agenda typically consisted of about 200 items, mostly minor, which were enumerated in charts placarded around the room. All sides were heard and decisions made. By the miracle of computerized text editing (and lots of fine staff work), each participant found an updated manual, embodying yesterday's decisions, at his seat every morning.

These "fall festivals" were useful not only for resolving decisions, but also for getting them accepted. Everyone was heard, everyone participated, everyone understood better the intricate constraints and interrelationships among decisions.

Multiple Implementations

System/360 architects had two almost unprecedented advantages: enough time to work carefully, and political clout equal to that of the implementers. The provision of enough time came from the schedule of the new technology; the political equality came from the simultaneous construction of multiple implementations. The necessity for strict compatibility among these served as the best possible enforcing agent for the specifications.

In most computer projects there comes a day when it is discovered that the machine and the manual don't agree. When the confrontation follows, the manual usually loses, for it can be changed far more quickly and cheaply than the machine. Not so, however, when there are multiple implementations. Then the delays and costs associated with fixing the errant machine can be overmatched by delays and costs in revising the machines that followed the manual faithfully.

This notion can be fruitfully applied whenever a programming language is being defined. One can be certain that several interpreters or compilers will sooner or later have to be built to meet various objectives. The definition will be cleaner and the discipline tighter if at least two implementations are built initially.

The Telephone Log

As implementation proceeds, countless questions of architectural interpretation arise, no matter how precise the specification. Obviously many such questions require amplifications and clarifications in the text. Others merely reflect misunderstandings.

It is essential, however, to encourage the puzzled implementer to telephone the responsible architect and ask his question, rather than to guess and proceed. It is just as vital to recognize that the answers to such questions are *ex cathedra* architectural pronouncements that must be told to everyone.

One useful mechanism is a *telephone log* kept by the architect. In it he records every question and every answer. Each week the logs of the several architects are concatenated, reproduced, and distributed to the users and implementers. While this mechanism is quite informal, it is both quick and comprehensive.

Product Test

The project manager's best friend is his daily adversary, the independent product-testing organization. This group checks machines and programs against specifications and serves as a devil's advocate, pinpointing every conceivable defect and discrepancy. Every development organization needs such an independent technical auditing group to keep it honest.

In the last analysis the customer is the independent auditor. In the merciless light of real use, every flaw will show. The product-testing group then is the surrogate customer, specialized for finding flaws. Time after time, the careful product tester will find places where the word didn't get passed, where the design decisions were not properly understood or accurately implemented. For this reason such a testing group is a necessary link in the chain by which the design word is passed, a link that needs to operate early and simultaneously with design.

7
Why Did the Tower of Babel Fail?

7

Why Did the Tower of Babel Fail?

Now the whole earth used only one language, with few words. On the occasion of a migration from the east, men discovered a plain in the land of Shinar, and settled there. Then they said to one another, "Come, let us make bricks, burning them well." So they used bricks for stone, and bitumen for mortar. Then they said, "Come, let us build ourselves a city with a tower whose top shall reach the heavens (thus making a name for ourselves), so that we may not be scattered all over the earth." Then the Lord came down to look at the city and tower which human beings had built. The Lord said, "They are just one people, and they all have the same language. If this is what they can do as a beginning, then nothing that they resolve to do will be impossible for them. Come, let us go down, and there make such a babble of their language that they will not understand one another's speech." Thus the Lord dispersed them from there all over the earth, so that they had to stop building the city.

GENESIS 11:1–8

P. Breughel, the Elder, "Turmbau zu Babel," 1563
Kunsthistorisches Museum, Vienna

A Management Audit of the Babel Project

According to the Genesis account, the tower of Babel was man's second major engineering undertaking, after Noah's ark. Babel was the first engineering fiasco.

The story is deep and instructive on several levels. Let us, however, examine it purely as an engineering project, and see what management lessons can be learned. How well was their project equipped with the prerequisites for success? Did they have:

1. A *clear mission?* Yes, although naively impossible. The project failed long before it ran into this fundamental limitation.
2. *Manpower?* Plenty of it.
3. *Materials?* Clay and asphalt are abundant in Mesopotamia.
4. Enough *time?* Yes, there is no hint of any time constraint.
5. Adequate *technology?* Yes, the pyramidal or conical structure is inherently stable and spreads the compressive load well. Clearly masonry was well understood. The project failed before it hit technological limitations.

Well, if they had all of these things, why did the project fail? Where did they lack? In two respects—*communication,* and its consequent, *organization.* They were unable to talk with each other; hence they could not coordinate. When coordination failed, work ground to a halt. Reading between the lines we gather that lack of communication led to disputes, bad feelings, and group jealousies. Shortly the clans began to move apart, preferring isolation to wrangling.

Communication in the Large Programming Project

So it is today. Schedule disaster, functional misfits, and system bugs all arise because the left hand doesn't know what the right hand is doing. As work proceeds, the several teams slowly change the functions, sizes, and speeds of their own programs, and they explicitly or implicitly change their assumptions about the inputs available and the uses to be made of the outputs.

For example, the implementer of a program-overlaying function may run into problems and reduce speed, relying on statistics that show how rarely this function will arise in application programs. Meanwhile, back at the ranch, his neighbor may be designing a major part of the supervisor so that it critically depends upon the speed of this function. This change in speed itself becomes a major specification change, and it needs to be proclaimed abroad and weighed from a system point of view.

How, then, shall teams communicate with one another? In as many ways as possible.

- *Informally.* Good telephone service and a clear definition of intergroup dependencies will encourage the hundreds of calls upon which common interpretation of written documents depends.

- *Meetings.* Regular project meetings, with one team after another giving technical briefings, are invaluable. Hundreds of minor misunderstandings get smoked out this way.

- *Workbook.* A formal project workbook must be started at the beginning. This deserves a section by itself.

The Project Workbook

What.   The project workbook is not so much a separate document as it is a structure imposed on the documents that the project will be producing anyway.

All the documents of the project need to be part of this structure. This includes objectives, external specifications, interface specifications, technical standards, internal specifications, and administrative memoranda.

Why.   Technical prose is almost immortal. If one examines the genealogy of a customer manual for a piece of hardware or software, one can trace not only the ideas, but also many of the very sentences and paragraphs back to the first memoranda proposing the product or explaining the first design. For the technical writer, the paste-pot is as mighty as the pen.

Since this is so, and since tomorrow's product-quality manuals will grow from today's memos, it is very important to get the structure of the documentation right. The early design of the project workbook ensures that the documentation structure itself is crafted, not haphazard. Moreover, the establishment of a structure molds later writing into segments that fit into that structure.

The second reason for the project workbook is control of the distribution of information. The problem is not to restrict information, but to ensure that relevant information gets to all the people who need it.

The first step is to number all memoranda, so that ordered lists of titles are available and each worker can see if he has what he wants. The organization of the workbook goes well beyond this to establish a tree-structure of memoranda. The tree-structure allows distribution lists to be maintained by subtree, if that is desirable.

Mechanics.   As with so many programming management problems, the technical memorandum problem gets worse nonlinearly as size increases. With 10 people, documents can simply be numbered. With 100 people, several linear sequences will often suffice. With 1000, scattered inevitably over several physical locations, the *need* for a structured workbook increases and the *size* of the workbook increases. How then shall the mechanics be handled?

I think this was well done on the OS/360 project. The need for a well-structured workbook was strongly urged by O. S. Locken, who had seen its effectiveness on his previous project, the 1410-7010 operating system.

We quickly decided that *each* programmer should see *all* the material, i.e., should have a copy of the workbook in his own office.

Of critical importance is timely updating. The workbook must be current. This is very difficult to do if whole documents must be retyped for changes. In a looseleaf book, however, only pages need to be changed. We had available a computer-driven text-editing system, and this proved invaluable for timely maintenance. Offset masters were prepared directly on the computer printer, and turnaround time was less than a day. The recipient of all these updated pages has an assimilation problem, however. When he first receives a changed page, he wants to know, "What has been changed?" When he later consults it, he wants to know, "What is the definition today?"

The latter need is met by the continually maintained document. Highlighting of changes requires other steps. First, one must mark changed text on the page, e.g., by a vertical bar in the margin alongside every altered line. Second, one needs to distribute with the new pages a short, separately written change summary that lists the changes and remarks on their significance.

Our project had not been under way six months before we hit another problem. The workbook was about five feet thick! If we had stacked up the 100 copies serving programmers in our offices in Manhattan's Time-Life Building, they would have towered above the building itself. Furthermore, the daily change distribution averaged two inches, some 150 pages to be interfiled in the whole. Maintenance of the workbook began to take a significant time from each workday.

At this point we switched to microfiche, a change that saved a million dollars, even allowing for the cost of a microfiche reader for each office. We were able to arrange excellent turnaround on microfiche production; the workbook shrank from three cubic feet to one-sixth of a cubic foot and, most significantly, updates appeared in hundred-page chunks, reducing the interfiling problem a hundredfold.

Microfiche has its drawbacks. From the manager's point of view the awkward interfiling of paper pages ensured that the changes were *read,* which was the purpose of the workbook. Microfiche would make workbook maintenance too easy, unless the update fiche are distributed with a paper document enumerating the changes.

Also, a microfiche cannot readily be highlighted, marked, and commented by the reader. Documents with which the reader has interacted are more effective for the author and more useful for the reader.

On balance I think the microfiche was a very happy mechanism, and I would recommend it over a paper workbook for very large projects.

How would one do it today?   With today's system technology available, I think the technique of choice is to keep the workbook on the direct-access file, marked with change bars and revision dates. Each user would consult it from a display terminal (typewriters are too slow). A change summary, prepared daily, would be stored in LIFO fashion at a fixed access point. The programmer would probably read that daily, but if he missed a day he would need only read longer the next day. As he read the change summary, he could interrupt to consult the changed text itself.

Notice that the workbook itself is not changed. It is still the assemblage of all project documentation, structured according to a careful design. The only change is in the mechanics of distribution and consultation. D. C. Engelbart and his colleagues at the Stanford Research Institute have built such a system and are using it to build and maintain documentation for the ARPA network.

D. L. Parnas of Carnegie-Mellon University has proposed a still more radical solution.[1] His thesis is that the programmer is most effective if shielded from, rather than exposed to the details of construction of system parts other than his own. This presupposes that all interfaces are completely and precisely defined. While that is definitely sound design, dependence upon its perfect accomplishment is a recipe for disaster. A good information system both exposes interface errors and stimulates their correction.

Organization in the Large Programming Project

If there are n workers on a project, there are $(n^2-n)/2$ interfaces across which there may be communication, and there are potentially almost 2^n teams within which coordination must occur. The purpose of organization is to reduce the amount of communication and coordination necessary; hence organization is a radical attack on the communication problems treated above.

The means by which communication is obviated are *division of labor* and *specialization of function*. The tree-like structure of organizations reflects the diminishing need for detailed communication when division and specialization of labor are applied.

In fact, a tree organization really arises as a structure of authority and responsibility. The principle that no man can serve two masters dictates that the authority structure be tree-like. But the communication structure is not so restricted, and the tree is a barely passable approximation to the communication structure, which is a network. The inadequacies of the tree approximation give rise to staff groups, task forces, committees, and even the matrix-type organization used in many engineering laboratories.

Let us consider a tree-like programming organization, and examine the essentials which any subtree must have in order to be effective. They are:

1. a mission
2. a producer
3. a technical director or architect
4. a schedule
5. a division of labor
6. interface definitions among the parts

All of this is obvious and conventional except the distinction between the producer and the technical director. Let us first consider the two roles, then their relationship.

What is the role of the producer? He assembles the team, divides the work, and establishes the schedule. He acquires and keeps on acquiring the necessary resources. This means that a major part of his role is communication outside the team, upwards and sideways. He establishes the pattern of communication and reporting within the team. Finally, he ensures that the schedule is met, shifting resources and organization to respond to changing circumstances.

How about the technical director? He conceives of the design to be built, identifies its subparts, specifies how it will look from outside, and sketches its internal structure. He provides unity and conceptual integrity to the whole design; thus he serves as a limit on system complexity. As individual technical problems arise, he invents solutions for them or shifts the system design as required. He is, in Al Capp's lovely phrase, "inside-man at the skunk works." His communications are chiefly within the team. His work is almost completely technical.

Now it is clear that the talents required for these two roles are quite different. Talents come in many different combinations; and the particular combination embodied in the producer and the director must govern the relationship between them. Organizations must be designed around the people available; not people fitted into pure-theory organizations.

Three relationships are possible, and all three are found in successful practice.

The producer and the technical director may be the same man. This is readily workable on very small teams, perhaps three to six programmers. On larger projects it is very rarely workable, for two reasons. First, the man with strong management talent and strong technical talent is rarely found. Thinkers are rare; doers are rarer; and thinker-doers are rarest.

Second, on the larger project each of the roles is necessarily a full-time job, or more. It is hard for the producer to delegate enough of his duties to give him any technical time. It is impossible for the director to delegate his without compromising the conceptual integrity of the design.

The producer may be boss, the director his right-hand man. The difficulty here is to establish the director's *authority* to make technical decisions without impacting his time as would putting him in the management chain-of-command.

Obviously the producer must proclaim the director's technical authority, and he must back it in an extremely high proportion of the test cases that will arise. For this to be possible, the producer and the director must see alike on fundamental technical philosophy; they must talk out the main technical issues privately, before they really become timely; and the producer must have a high respect for the director's technical prowess.

Less obviously, the producer can do all sorts of subtle things with the symbols of status (office size, carpet, furnishing, carbon copies, etc.) to proclaim that the director, although outside the management line, is a source of decision power.

This can be made to work very effectively. Unfortunately it is rarely tried. The job done least well by project managers is to utilize the technical genius who is not strong on management talent.

The director may be boss, and the producer his right-hand man. Robert Heinlein, in *The Man Who Sold the Moon*, describes such an arrangement in a graphic for-instance:

> *Coster buried his face in his hands, then looked up. "I know it. I know what needs to be done—but every time I try to tackle a technical problem some bloody fool wants me to make a decision about trucks —or telephones—or some damn thing. I'm sorry, Mr. Harriman. I thought I could do it."*
>
> *Harriman said very gently, "Don't let it throw you, Bob. You haven't had much sleep lately, have you? Tell you what—we'll put over a fast one on Ferguson. I'll take that desk you're at for a few days and build you a set-up to protect you against such things. I want that brain of yours thinking about reaction vectors and fuel efficiencies and design stresses, not about contracts for trucks." Harriman stepped to the door, looked around the outer office and spotted a man who might or might not be the office's chief clerk. "Hey you! C'mere."*
>
> *The man looked startled, got up, came to the door and said, "Yes?"*
>
> *"I want that desk in the corner and all the stuff that's on it moved to an empty office on this floor, right away."*

He supervised getting Coster and his other desk moved into another office, saw to it that the phone in the new office was disconnected, and, as an afterthought, had a couch moved in there, too. "We'll install a projector, and a drafting machine and bookcases and other junk like that tonight," he told Coster. "Just make a list of anything you need —to work on engineering." *He went back to the nominal chief-engineer's office and got happily to work trying to figure where the organization stood and what was wrong with it.*

Some four hours later he took Berkeley in to meet Coster. The chief engineer was asleep at his desk, head cradled on his arms. Harriman started to back out, but Coster roused. "Oh! Sorry," he said, blushing, "I must have dozed off."

"That's why I brought you the couch," said Harriman. "It's more restful. Bob, meet Jock Berkeley. He's your new slave. You remain chief engineer and top, undisputed boss. Jock is Lord High Everything Else. From now on you've got absolutely nothing to worry about— except for the little detail of building a Moon ship."

They shook hands. "Just one thing I ask, Mr. Coster," Berkeley said seriously, "bypass me all you want to—you'll have to run the technical show—but for God's sake record it so I'll know what's going on. I'm going to have a switch placed on your desk that will operate a sealed recorder at my desk."

"Fine!" Coster was looking, Harriman thought, younger already.

"And if you want something that is not technical, don't do it yourself. Just flip a switch and whistle; it'll get done!" Berkeley glanced at Harriman. "The Boss says he wants to talk with you about the real job. I'll leave you and get busy." He left.

Harriman sat down; Coster followed suit and said, "Whew!"

"Feel better?"

"I like the looks of that fellow Berkeley."

"That's good; he's your twin brother from now on. Stop worrying; I've used him before. You'll think you're living in a well-run hospital."[2]

This account hardly needs any analytic commentary. This arrangement, too, can be made to work effectively.

I suspect that the last arrangement is best for small teams, as discussed in Chapter 3, "The Surgical Team." I think the producer as boss is a more suitable arrangement for the larger subtrees of a really big project.

The Tower of Babel was perhaps the first engineering fiasco, but it was not the last. Communication and its consequent, organization, are critical for success. The techniques of communication and organization demand from the manager much thought and as much experienced competence as the software technology itself.

8
Calling the Shot

8
Calling the Shot

Practice is the best of all instructors.

PUBLILIUS

Experience is a dear teacher, but fools will learn at no other.

POOR RICHARD'S ALMANAC

Douglass Crockwell, "Ruth calls his shot," World Series, 1932
Reproduced by permission of Esquire Magazine and Douglass Crockwell, © 1945 (renewed 1973) by Esquire, Inc., and courtesy of the National Baseball Museum.

How long will a system programming job take? How much effort will be required? How does one estimate?

I have earlier suggested ratios that seem to apply to planning time, coding, component test, and system test. First, one must say that one does *not* estimate the entire task by estimating the coding portion only and then applying the ratios. The coding is only one-sixth or so of the problem, and errors in its estimate or in the ratios could lead to ridiculous'results.

Second, one must say that data for building isolated small programs are not applicable to programming systems products. For a program averaging about 3200 words, for example, Sackman, Erikson, and Grant report an average code-plus-debug time of about 178 hours for a single programmer, a figure which would extrapolate to give an annual productivity of 35,800 statements per year. A program half that size took less than one-fourth as long, and extrapolated productivity is almost 80,000 statements per year.[1] Planning, documentation, testing, system integration, and training times must be added. The linear extrapolation of such sprint figures is meaningless. Extrapolation of times for the hundred-yard dash shows that a man can run a mile in under three minutes.

Before dismissing them, however, let us note that these numbers, although not for strictly comparable problems, suggest that effort goes as a power of size *even* when no communication is involved except that of a man with his memories.

Figure 8.1 tells the sad story. It illustrates results reported from a study done by Nanus and Farr[2] at System Development Corporation. This shows an exponent of 1.5; that is,

$$\text{effort} = (\text{constant}) \times (\text{number of instructions})^{1.5}.$$

Another SDC study reported by Weinwurm[3] also shows an exponent near 1.5.

A few studies on programmer productivity have been made, and several estimating techniques have been proposed. Morin has prepared a survey of the published data.[4] Here I shall give only a few items that seem especially illuminating.

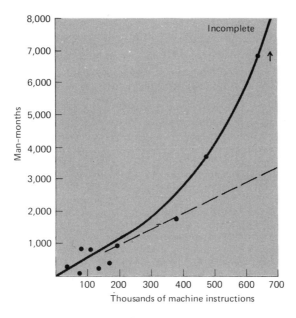

Fig. 8.1 Programming effort as a function of program size

Portman's Data

Charles Portman, manager of ICL's Software Division, Computer Equipment Organization (Northwest) at Manchester, offers another useful personal insight.[5]

He found his programming teams missing schedules by about one-half—each job was taking approximately twice as long as estimated. The estimates were very careful, done by experienced teams estimating man-hours for several hundred subtasks on a PERT chart. When the slippage pattern appeared, he asked them to keep careful daily logs of time usage. These showed that the estimating error could be entirely accounted for by the fact that his teams were only realizing 50 percent of the working week as actual programming and debugging time. Machine downtime, higher-priority short unrelated jobs, meetings, paperwork, company business, sickness, personal time, etc. accounted for the rest. In short, the estimates made an unrealistic assumption about the number of technical work hours per man-year. My own experience quite confirms his conclusion.[6]

Aron's Data

Joel Aron, manager of Systems Technology at IBM in Gaithersburg, Maryland, has studied programmer productivity when working on nine large systems (briefly, *large* means more than 25 programmers and 30,000 deliverable instructions).[7] He divides such systems according to interactions among programmers (and system parts) and finds productivities as follows:

> Very few interactions   10,000 instructions per man-year
> Some interactions   5,000
> Many interactions   1,500

The man-years do not include support and system test activities, only design and programming. When these figures are diluted by a factor of two to cover system test, they closely match Harr's data.

Harr's Data

John Harr, manager of programming for the Bell Telephone Laboratories' Electronic Switching System, reported his and others' experience in a paper at the 1969 Spring Joint Computer Conference.[8] These data are shown in Figs. 8.2, 8.3, and 8.4.

Of these, Fig. 8.2 is the most detailed and the most useful. The first two jobs are basically control programs; the second two are basically language translators. Productivity is stated in terms of debugged words per man-year. This includes programming, component test, and system test. It is not clear how much of the planning effort, or effort in machine support, writing, and the like, is included.

	Prog. units	Number of programmers	Years	Man-years	Program words	Words/ man-yr.
Operational	50	83	4	101	52,000	515
Maintenance	36	60	4	81	51,000	630
Compiler	13	9	2¼	17	38,000	2230
Translator (Data assembler)	15	13	2½	11	25,000	2270

Fig. 8.2   Summary of four No. 1 ESS program jobs

The productivities likewise fall into two classifications; those for control programs are about 600 words per man-year; those for translators are about 2200 words per man-year. Note that all four programs are of similar size—the variation is in size of the work groups, length of time, and number of modules. Which is cause and which is effect? Did the control programs require more people because they were more complicated? Or did they require more modules and more man-months because they were assigned more people? Did they take longer because of the greater complexity, or because more people were assigned? One can't be sure. The control programs were surely more complex. These uncertainties aside, the numbers describe the real productivities achieved on a large system, using present-day programming techniques. As such they are a real contribution.

Figures 8.3 and 8.4 show some interesting data on programming and debugging rates as compared to predicted rates.

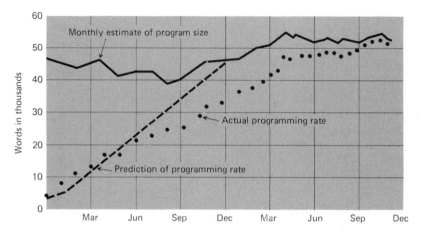

Fig. 8.3   ESS predicted and actual programming rates

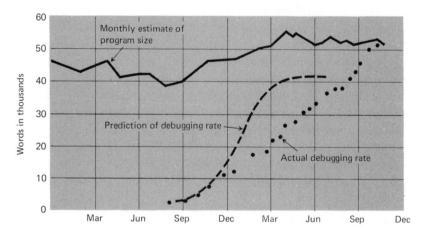

Fig. 8.4   ESS predicted and actual debugging rates

OS/360 Data

IBM OS/360 experience, while not available in the detail of Harr's data, confirms it. Productivities in range of 600–800 debugged instructions per man-year were experienced by control program groups. Productivities in the 2000–3000 debugged instructions per man-year were achieved by language translator groups. These include planning done by the group, coding component test, system test, and some support activities. They are comparable to Harr's data, so far as I can tell.

Aron's data, Harr's data, and the OS/360 data all confirm striking differences in productivity related to the complexity and difficulty of the task itself. My guideline in the morass of estimating complexity is that compilers are three times as bad as normal batch application programs, and operating systems are three times as bad as compilers.[9]

Corbató's Data

Both Harr's data and OS/360 data are for assembly language programming. Little data seem to have been published on system programming productivity using higher-level languages. Corbató of MIT's Project MAC reports, however, a mean productivity of 1200 lines of debugged PL/I statements per man-year on the MULTICS system (between 1 and 2 million words).[10]

This number is very exciting. Like the other projects, MULTICS includes control programs and language translators. Like the others, it is producing a system programming product, tested and documented. The data seem to be comparable in terms of kind of effort included. And the productivity number is a good average between the control program and translator productivities of other projects.

But Corbató's number is *lines* per man-year, not *words*! Each statement in his system corresponds to about three to five words of handwritten code! This suggests two important conclusions.

- Productivity seems constant in terms of elementary statements, a conclusion that is reasonable in terms of the thought a statement requires and the errors it may include.[11]
- Programming productivity may be increased as much as five times when a suitable high-level language is used.[12]

9
Ten Pounds in a Five-Pound Sack

9

Ten Pounds
in a Five-Pound Sack

*The author should gaze at Noah, and . . . learn, as they
did in the Ark, to crowd a great deal of matter into a very
small compass.*

SYDNEY SMITH, EDINBURGH REVIEW

Engraved from a painting by Heywood Hardy
The Bettman Archive

Program Space as Cost

How big is it? Aside from running time, the space occupied by a program is a principal cost. This is true even for proprietary programs, where the user pays the author a fee that is essentially a share of the development cost. Consider the IBM APL interactive software system. It rents for $400 per month and, when used, takes at least 160 K bytes of memory. On a Model 165, memory rents for about $12 per kilobyte per month. If the program is available full-time, one pays $400 software rent and $1920 memory rent for using the program. If one uses the APL system only four hours a day, the costs are $400 software rent and $320 memory rent per month.

One frequently hears horror expressed that a 2 M byte machine may have 400 K devoted to its operating system. This is as foolish as criticizing a Boeing 747 because it costs $27 million. One must also ask, "What does it do?" What does one get in ease-of-use and in performance (via efficient system utilization) for the dollars so spent? Could the $4800 per month thus invested in memory rental have been more fruitfully spent for other hardware, for programmers, for application programs?

The system designer puts part of his total hardware resource into resident-program memory when he thinks it will do more for the user in that form than as adders, disks, etc. To do otherwise would be grossly irresponsible. And the result must be judged as a whole. No one can criticize a programming system for size *per se* and at the same time consistently advocate closer integration of hardware and software design.

Since size is such a large part of the user cost of a programming system product, the builder must set size targets, control size, and devise size-reduction techniques, just as the hardware builder sets component-count targets, controls component count, and devises count-reduction techniques. Like any cost, size itself is not bad, but unnecessary size is.

Size Control

For the project manager, size control is partly a technical job and partly a managerial one. One has to study users and their applications to set the sizes of the systems to be offered. Then these systems have to be subdivided, and each component given a size target. Since size-speed trade-offs come in rather big quantum jumps, setting size targets is a tricky business, requiring knowledge of the available trade-offs within each piece. The wise manager also saves himself a kitty, to be allocated as work proceeds.

In OS/360, even though all of this was done very carefully, still other lessons had to be painfully learned.

First, setting size targets for core is not enough; one has to budget all aspects of size. In most previous operating systems, systems residence had been on tape, and the long search times of tape meant that one was not tempted to use it casually to bring in program segments. OS/360 was disk-resident, like its immediate predecessors, the Stretch Operating System and the 1410-7010 Disk Operating System. Its builders rejoiced in the freedom of cheap disk accesses. The initial result was disastrous to performance.

In setting core sizes for each component, we had not simultaneously set access budgets. As anyone with 20–20 hindsight would expect, a programmer who found his program slopping over his core target broke it into overlays. This process in itself added to the total size and slowed execution down. Most seriously, our management control system neither measured nor caught this. Each man reported as to how much *core* he was using, and since he was within target, no one worried.

Fortunately, there came a day early in the effort when the OS/360 performance simulator began to work. The first result indicated deep trouble. Fortran H, on a Model 65 with drums, simulated compiling at five statements per minute! Digging-in showed that the control program modules were each making many, many disk accesses. Even high-frequency supervisor modules were making many trips to the well, and the result was quite analogous to page thrashing.

The first moral is clear: Set *total* size budgets as well as resident-space budgets; set budgets on backing-store accesses as well as on sizes.

The next lesson was very similar. The space budgets were set before precise functional allocations were made to each module. As a result, any programmer in size trouble examined his code to see what he could throw over the fence into a neighbor's space. So buffers managed by the control program became part of the user's space. More seriously, so did all kinds of control blocks, and the effect was utterly compromising to the security and protection of the system.

So the second moral is also clear: Define exactly what a module must do when you specify how big it must be.

A third and deeper lesson shows through these experiences. The project was large enough and management communication poor enough to prompt many members of the team to see themselves as contestants making brownie points, rather than as builders making programming products. Each suboptimized his piece to meet his targets; few stopped to think about the total effect on the customer. This breakdown in orientation and communication is a major hazard for large projects. All during implementation, the system architects must maintain continual vigilance to ensure continued system integrity. Beyond this policing mechanism, however, lies the matter of attitude of the implementers themselves. Fostering a total-system, user-oriented attitude may well be the most important function of the programming manager.

Space Techniques

No amount of space budgeting and control can make a program small. That requires invention and craftsmanship.

Obviously, more function means more space, speed being held constant. So the first area of craftsmanship is in trading function for size. Here there comes an early and deep policy question. How much of that choice shall be reserved for the user? One can design a program with many optional features, each of which takes a little space. One can design a generator that will take an option list and tailor a program to it. But for any particular set of options, a more monolithic program would take less space. It's rather like a car; if the map light, cigarette lighter, and clock are priced together as a single option, the package will cost less than if one can choose each separately. So the designer must decide how fine-grained the user choice of options will be.

In designing a system for a range of memory sizes, another basic question arises. A limiting effect keeps the range of suitability from being made arbitrarily wide, even with fine-grained modularity of function. In the smallest system, most modules will be overlaid. A substantial part of the smallest system's resident space must be set aside as a transient or paging area into which other parts are fetched. The size of this determines the size of all modules. And breaking functions into small modules costs both performance and space. So a large system, which can afford a transient area twenty times as large, only saves accesses thereby. It still suffers in both speed and space because the module size is so small. This effect limits the maximum efficient system that can be generated from the modules of a small system.

The second area of craftsmanship is space-time trade-offs. For a given function, the more space, the faster. This is true over an amazingly large range. It is this fact that makes it feasible to set space budgets.

The manager can do two things to help his team make good space-time trade-offs. One is to ensure that they are trained in programming technique, not just left to rely on native wit and previous experience. For a new language or machine this is especially important. The peculiarities of its skillful use need to be learned quickly and shared widely, perhaps with special prizes or praises for new techniques.

The second is to recognize that programming has a technology, and components need to be fabricated. Every project needs a notebook full of good subroutines or macros for queuing, searching, hashing, and sorting. For each such function the notebook should have at least two programs, the quick and the squeezed. The development of such technology is an important realization task that can be done in parallel with system architecture.

Representation Is the Essence of Programming

Beyond craftsmanship lies invention, and it is here that lean, spare, fast programs are born. Almost always these are the result of stategic breakthrough rather than tactical cleverness. Sometimes the strategic breakthrough will be a new algorithm, such as the Cooley-Tukey Fast Fourier Transform or the substitution of an $n \log n$ sort for an n^2 set of comparisons.

Much more often, strategic breakthrough will come from redoing the representation of the data or tables. This is where the heart of a program lies. Show me your flowcharts and conceal your tables, and I shall continue to be mystified. Show me your tables, and I won't usually need your flowcharts; they'll be obvious.

It is easy to multiply examples of the power of representations. I recall a young man undertaking to build an elaborate console interpreter for an IBM 650. He ended up packing it onto an incredibly small amount of space by building an interpreter for the interpreter, recognizing that human interactions are slow and infrequent, but space was dear. Digitek's elegant little Fortran compiler uses a very dense, specialized representation for the compiler code itself, so that external storage is not needed. That time lost in decoding this representation is gained back tenfold by avoiding input-output. (The exercises at the end of Chapter 6 in Brooks and Iverson, *Automatic Data Processing*[1] include a collection of such examples, as do many of Knuth's exercises.[2])

The programmer at wit's end for lack of space can often do best by disentangling himself from his code, rearing back, and contemplating his data. Representation *is* the essence of programming.

10
The Documentary Hypothesis

10

The Documentary Hypothesis

The hypothesis:

Amid a wash of paper, a small number of documents become the critical pivots around which every project's management revolves. These are the manager's chief personal tools.

The technology, the surrounding organization, and the traditions of the craft conspire to define certain items of paperwork that a project must prepare. To the new manager, fresh from operating as a craftsman himself, these seem an unmitigated nuisance, an unnecessary distraction, and a white tide that threatens to engulf him. And indeed, most of them are exactly that.

Bit by bit, however, he comes to realize that a certain small set of these documents embodies and expresses much of his managerial work. The preparation of each one serves as a major occasion for focusing thought and crystallizing discussions that otherwise would wander endlessly. Its maintenance becomes his surveillance and warning mechanism. The document itself serves as a check list, a status control, and a data base for his reporting.

In order to see how this should work for a software project, let us examine the specific documents useful in other contexts and see if a generalization emerges.

Documents for a Computer Product

Suppose one is building a machine. What are the critical documents?

Objectives.   This defines the need to be met and the goals, desiderata, constraints, and priorities.

Specifications.   This is a computer manual plus performance specifications. It is one of the first documents generated in proposing a new product, and the last document finished.

Schedule

Budget.   Not merely a constraint, the budget is one of the manager's most useful documents. Existence of the budget forces technical decisions that otherwise would be avoided; and, more important, it forces and clarifies policy decisions.

Organization chart

Space allocations

Estimate, forecast, prices. These three have cyclic interlocking, which determines the success or failure of the project:

To generate a market forecast, one needs performance specifications and postulated prices. The quantities from the forecast combine with component counts from the design to determine the manufacturing cost estimate, and they determine the per-unit share of development and fixed costs. These costs in turn determine prices.

If the prices are *below* those postulated, a joyous success spiral begins. Forecasts rise, unit costs drop, and prices drop yet further.

If the prices are *above* those postulated, a disastrous spiral begins, and all hands must struggle to break it. Performance must be squeezed up and new applications developed to support larger forecasts. Costs must be squeezed down to yield lower estimates. The stress of this cycle is a discipline that often evokes the best work of marketer and engineer.

It can also bring about ridiculous vacillation. I recall a machine whose instruction counter popped in or out of memory every six months during a three-year development cycle. At one phase a little more performance would be wanted, so the instruction counter was implemented in transistors. At the next phase cost reduction was the theme, so the counter would be implemented as a memory location. On another project the best engineering manager I ever saw served often as a giant flywheel, his inertia damping the fluctuations that came from market and management people.

Documents for a University Department

In spite of the immense differences in purpose and activity, a similar number of similar documents form the critical set for the chairman of a university department. Almost every decision by dean, faculty meeting, or chairman is a specification or change of these documents:

Objectives

Course descriptions

Degree requirements

Research proposals (hence plans, when funded)

Class schedule and teaching assignments

Budget

Space allocation

Assignment of staff and graduate students

Notice that the components are very like those of the computer project: objectives, product specifications, time allocations, money allocations, space allocations, and people allocations. Only the pricing documents are missing; here the legislature does that task. The similarities are not accidental—the concerns of any management task are what, when, how much, where, and who.

Documents for a Software Project

In many software projects, people begin by holding meetings to debate structure; then they start writing programs. No matter how small the project, however, the manager is wise to begin immediately to formalize at least mini-documents to serve as his data base. And he turns out to need documents much like those of other managers.

What: objectives.   This defines the need to be met and the goals, desiderata, constraints, and priorities.

What: product specifications.   This begins as a proposal and ends up as the manual and internal documentation. Speed and space specifications are a critical part.

When: schedule

How much: budget

Where: space allocation

Who: organization chart. This becomes intertwined with the interface specification, as Conway's Law predicts: "Organizations which design systems are constrained to produce systems which are copies of the communication structures of these organizations."[1] Conway goes on to point out that the organization chart will initially reflect the first system design, which is almost surely not the right one. If the system design is to be free to change, the organization must be prepared to change.

Why Have Formal Documents?

First, writing the decisions down is essential. Only when one writes do the gaps appear and the inconsistencies protrude. The act of writing turns out to require hundreds of mini-decisions, and it is the existence of these that distinguishes clear, exact policies from fuzzy ones.

Second, the documents will communicate the decisions to others. The manager will be continually amazed that policies he took for common knowledge are totally unknown by some member of his team. Since his fundamental job is to keep everybody going in the same direction, his chief daily task will be communication, not decision-making, and his documents will immensely lighten this load.

Finally, a manager's documents give him a data base and checklist. By reviewing them periodically he sees where he is, and he sees what changes of emphasis or shifts in direction are needed.

I do not share the salesman-projected vision of the "management total-information system," wherein the executive strokes an inquiry into a computer, and a display screen flashes his answer. There are many fundamental reasons why this will never happen.

One reason is that only a small part—perhaps 20 percent—of the executive's time is spent on tasks where he needs information from outside his head. The rest is communication: hearing, reporting, teaching, exhorting, counseling, encouraging. But for the fraction that *is* data-based, the handful of critical documents are vital, and they will meet almost all needs.

The task of the manager is to develop a plan and then to realize it. But only the written plan is precise and communicable. Such a plan consists of documents on what, when, how much, where, and who. This small set of critical documents encapsulates much of the manager's work. If their comprehensive and critical nature is recognized in the beginning, the manager can approach them as friendly tools rather than annoying busywork. He will set his direction much more crisply and quickly by doing so.

11
Plan to Throw
One Away

11
Plan to Throw One Away

There is nothing in this world constant but inconstancy.

SWIFT

It is common sense to take a method and try it. If it fails, admit it frankly and try another. But above all, try something.

FRANKLIN D. ROOSEVELT[1]

Collapse of the aerodynamically misdesigned Tacoma Narrows Bridge, 1940
UPI Photo/The Bettman Archive

Pilot Plants and Scaling Up

Chemical engineers learned long ago that a process that works in the laboratory cannot be implemented in a factory in only one step. An intermediate step called the *pilot plant* is necessary to give experience in scaling quantities up and in operating in nonprotective environments. For example, a laboratory process for desalting water will be tested in a pilot plant of 10,000 gallon/day capacity before being used for a 2,000,000 gallon/day community water system.

Programming system builders have also been exposed to this lesson, but it seems to have not yet been learned. Project after project designs a set of algorithms and then plunges into construction of customer-deliverable software on a schedule that demands delivery of the first thing built.

In most projects, the first system built is barely usable. It may be too slow, too big, awkward to use, or all three. There is no alternative but to start again, smarting but smarter, and build a redesigned version in which these problems are solved. The discard and redesign may be done in one lump, or it may be done piece-by-piece. But all large-system experience shows that it will be done.[2] Where a new system concept or new technology is used, one has to build a system to throw away, for even the best planning is not so omniscient as to get it right the first time.

The management question, therefore, is not *whether* to build a pilot system and throw it away. You *will* do that. The only question is whether to plan in advance to build a throwaway, or to promise to deliver the throwaway to customers. Seen this way, the answer is much clearer. Delivering that throwaway to customers buys time, but it does so only at the cost of agony for the user, distraction for the builders while they do the redesign, and a bad reputation for the product that the best redesign will find hard to live down.

Hence *plan to throw one away; you will, anyhow.*

The Only Constancy Is Change Itself

Once one recognizes that a pilot system must be built and discarded, and that a redesign with changed ideas is inevitable, it becomes useful to face the whole phenomenon of change. The first step is to accept the fact of change as a way of life, rather than an untoward and annoying exception. Cosgrove has perceptively pointed out that the programmer delivers satisfaction of a user need rather than any tangible product. And both the actual need and the user's perception of that need will change as programs are built, tested, and used.[3]

Of course this is also true of the needs met by hardware products, whether new cars or new computers. But the very existence of a tangible object serves to contain and quantize user demand for changes. Both the tractability and the invisibility of the software product expose its builders to perpetual changes in requirements.

Far be it from me to suggest that all changes in customer objectives and requirements must, can, or should be incorporated in the design. Clearly a threshold has to be established, and it must get higher and higher as development proceeds, or no product ever appears.

Nevertheless, some changes in objectives are inevitable, and it is better to be prepared for them than to assume that they won't come. Not only are changes in objective inevitable, changes in development strategy and technique are also inevitable. The throw-one-away concept is itself just an acceptance of the fact that as one learns, he changes the design.[4]

Plan the System for Change

The ways of designing a system for such change are well known and widely discussed in the literature—perhaps more widely discussed than practiced. They include careful modularization, extensive subroutining, precise and complete definition of intermodule interfaces, and complete documentation of these. Less obviously one wants standard calling sequences and table-driven techniques used wherever possible.

Most important is the use of a high-level language and self-documenting techniques so as to reduce errors induced by changes. Using compile-time operations to incorporate standard declarations helps powerfully in making changes.

Quantization of change is an essential technique. Every product should have numbered versions, and each version must have its own schedule and a freeze date, after which changes go into the next version.

Plan the Organization for Change

Cosgrove advocates treating all plans, milestones, and schedules as tentative, so as to facilitate change. This goes much too far—the common failing of programming groups today is too little management control, not too much.

Nevertheless, he offers a great insight. He observes that the reluctance to document designs is not due merely to laziness or time pressure. Instead it comes from the designer's reluctance to commit himself to the defense of decisions which he knows to be tentative. "By documenting a design, the designer exposes himself to the criticisms of everyone, and he must be able to defend everything he writes. If the organizational structure is threatening in any way, nothing is going to be documented until it is completely defensible."

Structuring an organization for change is much harder than designing a system for change. Each man must be assigned to jobs that broaden him, so that the whole force is technically flexible. On a large project the manager needs to keep two or three top programmers as a technical cavalry that can gallop to the rescue wherever the battle is thickest.

Management structures also need to be changed as the system changes. This means that the boss must give a great deal of attention to keeping his managers and his technical people as interchangeable as their talents allow.

The barriers are sociological, and they must be fought with constant vigilance. First, managers themselves often think of senior people as "too valuable" to use for actual programming. Next, management jobs carry higher prestige. To overcome this problem some laboratories, such as Bell Labs, abolish all job titles. Each professional employee is a "member of the technical staff." Others, like IBM, maintain a dual ladder of advancement, as Fig. 11.1 shows. The corresponding rungs are in theory equivalent.

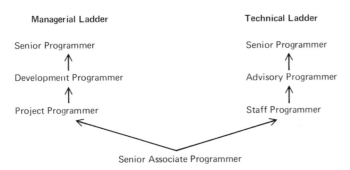

Fig. 11.1   IBM dual ladder of advancement

It is easy to establish corresponding salary scales for rungs. It is much harder to give them corresponding prestige. Offices have to be of equal size and appointment. Secretarial and other support services must correspond. A reassignment from the technical ladder to a corresponding level on the managerial one should never be accompanied by a raise, and it should be announced always as a "reassignment," never as a "promotion." The reverse reassignment should always carry a raise; overcompensating for the cultural forces is necessary.

Managers need to be sent to technical refresher courses, senior technical people to management training. Project objectives, progress, and management problems must be shared with the whole body of senior people.

Whenever talents permit, senior people must be kept technically and emotionally ready to manage groups or to delight in building programs with their own hands. Doing this surely is a lot of work; but it surely is worth it!

The whole notion of organizing surgical-type programming teams is a radical attack on this problem. It has the effect of making a senior man feel that he does not demean himself when he builds programs, and it attempts to remove the social obstacles that deprive him of that creative joy.

Furthermore, that structure is designed to minimize the number of interfaces. As such, it makes the system maximally easy to change, and it becomes relatively easy to reassign a whole surgical team to a different programming task when organizational changes are necessary. It is really the long-run answer to the problem of flexible organization.

Two Steps Forward and One Step Back

A program doesn't stop changing when it is delivered for customer use. The changes after delivery are called *program maintenance,* but the process is fundamentally different from hardware maintenance.

Hardware maintenance for a computer system involves three activities—replacing deteriorated components, cleaning and lubricating, and putting in engineering changes that fix design defects. (Most, but not all, engineering changes fix defects in the realization or implementation, rather than the architecture, and so are invisible to the user.)

Program maintenance involves no cleaning, lubrication, or repair of deterioration. It consists chiefly of changes that repair design defects. Much more often than with hardware, these changes include added functions. Usually they are visible to the user.

The total cost of maintaining a widely used program is typically 40 percent or more of the cost of developing it. Surprisingly, this cost is strongly affected by the number of users. More users find more bugs.

Betty Campbell, of MIT's Laboratory for Nuclear Science, points out an interesting cycle in the life of a particular release of a program. It is shown in Fig. 11.2. Initially, old bugs found and solved in previous releases tend to reappear in a new release. New functions of the new release turn out to have defects. These things get shaken out, and all goes well for several months. Then the bug rate begins to climb again. Miss Campbell believes this is due to the arrival of users at a new plateau of sophistication, where they begin to exercise fully the new capabilities of the release. This intense workout then smokes out the more subtle bugs in the new features.[5]

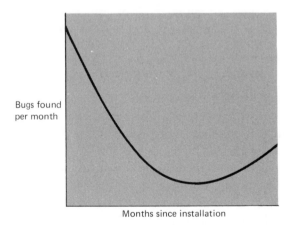

Bugs found
per month

Months since installation

Fig. 11.2 Bug occurrence as a function of release age

The fundamental problem with program maintenance is that fixing a defect has a substantial (20–50 percent) chance of introducing another. So the whole process is two steps forward and one step back.

Why aren't defects fixed more cleanly? First, even a subtle defect shows itself as a local failure of some kind. In fact it often has system-wide ramifications, usually nonobvious. Any attempt to fix it with minimum effort will repair the local and obvious, but unless the structure is pure or the documentation very fine, the far-reaching effects of the repair will be overlooked. Second, the repairer is usually not the man who wrote the code, and often he is a junior programmer or trainee.

As a consequence of the introduction of new bugs, program maintenance requires far more system testing per statement written than any other programming. Theoretically, after each fix one must run the entire bank of test cases previously run against the system, to ensure that it has not been damaged in an obscure way. In practice such *regression testing* must indeed approximate this theoretical ideal, and it is very costly.

Clearly, methods of designing programs so as to eliminate or at least illuminate side effects can have an immense payoff in maintenance costs. So can methods of implementing designs with fewer people, fewer interfaces, and hence fewer bugs.

One Step Forward and One Step Back

Lehman and Belady have studied the history of successive releases in a large operating system.[6] They find that the total number of modules increases linearly with release number, but that the number of modules affected increases exponentially with release number. All repairs tend to destroy the structure, to increase the entropy and disorder of the system. Less and less effort is spent on fixing original design flaws; more and more is spent on fixing flaws introduced by earlier fixes. As time passes, the system becomes less and less well-ordered. Sooner or later the fixing ceases to gain any ground. Each forward step is matched by a backward one. Although in principle usable forever, the system has worn out as a base for progress. Furthermore, machines change, configurations change, and user requirements change, so the system is not in fact usable forever. A brand-new, from-the-ground-up redesign is necessary.

And so from a statistical mechanical model, Belady and Lehman arrive for programming-systems at a more general conclusion supported by the experience of all the earth. "Things are always at their best in the beginning," said Pascal. C. S. Lewis has stated it more perceptively:

> *That is the key to history. Terrific energy is expended—civilizations are built up—excellent institutions devised; but each time something goes wrong. Some fatal flaw always brings the selfish and cruel people to the top, and then it all slides back into misery and ruin. In fact, the machine conks. It seems to start up all right and runs a few yards, and then it breaks down.* [7]

Systems program building is an entropy-decreasing process, hence inherently metastable. Program maintenance is an entropy-increasing process, and even its most skillful execution only delays the subsidence of the system into unfixable obsolescence.

12
Sharp Tools

12
Sharp Tools

A good workman is known by his tools.

PROVERB

A. Pisano, "Lo Scultore," from the Campanile di Santa Maria del Fiore, Florence, c. 1335
Scala/Art Resource, NY

Even at this late date, many programming projects are still operated like machine shops so far as tools are concerned. Each master mechanic has his own personal set, collected over a lifetime and carefully locked and guarded—the visible evidences of personal skills. Just so, the programmer keeps little editors, sorts, binary dumps, disk space utilities, etc., stashed away in his file.

Such an approach, however, is foolish for a programming project. First, the essential problem is communication, and individualized tools hamper rather than aid communication. Second, the technology changes when one changes machines or working language, so tool lifetime is short. Finally, it is obviously much more efficient to have common development and maintenance of the general-purpose programming tools.

General-purpose tools are not enough, however. Both specialized needs and personal preferences dictate the need for specialized tools as well; so in discussing programming teams I have postulated one toolmaker per team. This man masters all the common tools and is able to instruct his client-boss in their use. He also builds the specialized tools his boss needs.

The manager of a project, then, needs to establish a philosophy and set aside resources for the building of common tools. At the same time he must recognize the need for specialized tools, and not begrudge his working teams their own tool-building. This temptation is insidious. One feels that if all those scattered tool builders were gathered in to augment the common tool team, greater efficiency would result. But it is not so.

What are the tools about which the manager must philosophize, plan, and organize? First, a *computer facility*. This requires machines, and a scheduling philosophy must be adopted. It requires an *operating system,* and service philosophies must be established. It requires *language,* and a language policy must be laid down. Then there are *utilities, debugging aids, test-case generators,* and a *text-processing system* to handle documentation. Let us look at these one by one.[1]

Target Machines

Machine support is usefully divided into the *target machine* and the *vehicle machines.* The target machine is the one for which software is being written, and on which it must ultimately be tested. The vehicle machines are those that provide the services used in building the system. If one is building a new operating system for an old machine, it may serve not only as the target, but as the vehicle as well.

What kind of target facility?   Teams building new supervisors or other system-heart software will of course need machines of their own. Such systems will need operators and a system programmer or two who keeps the standard support on the machine current and serviceable.

If a separate machine is needed, it is a rather peculiar thing—it need not be fast, but it needs at least a million bytes of main storage, a hundred million bytes of on-line disk, and terminals. Only alphanumeric terminals are needed, but they must go much faster than the 15 characters per second that characterizes typewriters. A large memory adds greatly to productivity by allowing overlaying and size trimming to be done after functional testing.

The debugging machine, or its software, also needs to be instrumented, so that counts and measurements of all kinds of program parameters can be automatically made during debugging. Memory-use patterns, for instance, are powerful diagnostics of the causes of weird logical behavior or unexpectedly slow performance.

Scheduling.   When the target machine is new, as when its first operating system is being built, machine time is scarce, and scheduling it is a major problem. The requirement for target machine time has a peculiar growth curve. In OS/360 development we had good System/360 simulators and other vehicles. From previous experience we projected how many hours of S/360 time we would need, and began to acquire early machines from factory production. But they sat idle, month after month. Then all at once all 16 systems were fully loaded, and rationing was the problem. The utilization looked something like Fig. 12.1. Everyone began to debug his first components at the same time, and thereafter most of the team was constantly debugging something.

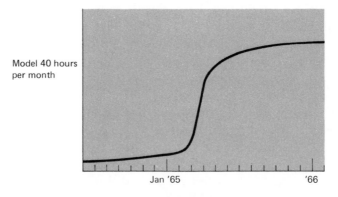

Fig. 12.1   Growth in use of target machines

We centralized all our machines and tape library and set up a professional and experienced machine-room team to run them. To maximize scarce S/360 time, we ran all debugging runs in batch on whichever system was free and appropriate. We tried for four shots per day (two-and-one-half-hour turnaround) and demanded four-hour turnaround. An auxiliary 1401 with terminals was used to schedule runs, to keep track of the thousands of jobs, and to monitor turnaround time.

But all that organization was quite overdone. After a few months of slow turnaround, mutual recriminations, and other agony, we went to allocating machine time in substantial blocks.

The whole fifteen-man sort team, for example, would be given a system for a four-to-six-hour block. It was up to them to schedule themselves on it. If it sat idle, no outsider could use it.

That, it develops, was a better way to allocate and schedule. Although machine utilization may have been a little lower (and often it wasn't), productivity was way up. For each man on such a team, ten shots in a six-hour block are far more productive than ten shots spaced three hours apart, because sustained concentration reduces thinking time. After such a sprint, a team usually needed a day or two to catch up on the paperwork before asking for another block. Often as few as three programmers can fruitfully share and subschedule a block of time. This seems to be the best way to use a target machine when debugging a new operating system.

It has always been so in practice, though never in theory. System debugging has always been a graveyard-shift occupation, like astronomy. Twenty years ago, on the 701, I was initiated into the productive informality of the predawn hours, when all the machine-room bosses are fast asleep at home, and the operators are disinclined to be sticklers for rules. Three machine generations have passed; technologies have changed totally; operating systems have arisen; and yet this preferred method of working hasn't changed. It endures because it is most productive. The time has come to recognize its productivity and embrace the fruitful practice openly.

Vehicle Machines and Data Services

Simulators.   If the target computer is new, one needs a logical simulator for it. This gives a debugging vehicle long before the real target exists. Equally important, it gives access to a *dependable* debugging vehicle even after one has a target machine available.

Dependable is not the same as *accurate.* The simulator will surely fail in some respect to be a faithful and accurate implementation of the new machine's architecture. But it will be the *same* implementation from one day to the next, and the new hardware will not.

We are accustomed nowadays to having computer hardware work correctly almost all the time. Unless an application programmer sees a system behaving inconsistently from run to identical run, he is well advised to look for bugs in his code rather than in his engine.

This experience, however, is bad training for the programming of support for a new machine. Lab-built, preproduction, or early hardware does *not* work as defined, does *not* work reliably, and does *not* stay the same from day to day. As bugs are found, engineering changes are made in all machine copies, including those of the programming group. This shifting base is bad enough. Hardware failures, usually intermittent, are worse. The uncertainty is worst of all, for it robs one of incentive to dig diligently in his code for a bug—it may not be there at all. So a dependable simulator on a well-aged vehicle retains its usefulness far longer than one would expect.

Compiler and assembler vehicles.   For the same reasons, one wants compilers and assemblers that run on dependable vehicles but compile object code for the target system. This can then start being debugged on the simulator.

With high-level language programming, one can do much of the debugging by compiling for and testing object code on the vehicle machine before beginning to test target-machine code at all. This gives the efficiency of direct execution, rather than that of simulation, combined with the dependability of the stable machine.

Program libraries and accounting.   A very successful and important use of a vehicle machine in the OS/360 development effort was for the maintenance of program libraries. A system developed under the leadership of W. R. Crowley had two 7010's connected, sharing a large disk data bank. The 7010's also provided an S/360 assembler. All the code tested or under test was kept in this library, both source code and assembled load modules. The library was in fact divided into sublibraries with different access rules.

First, each group or programmer had an area where he kept copies of his programs, his test cases, and the scaffolding he needed for component testing. In this *playpen* area there were no restrictions on what a man could do with his own programs; they were his.

When a man had his component ready for integration into a larger piece, he passed a copy over to the manager of that larger system, who put this copy into a *system integration sublibrary*. Now the original programmer could not change it, except by permission of the integration manager. As the system came together, the latter would proceed with all sorts of system tests, identifying bugs and getting fixes.

From time to time a system version would be ready for wider use. Then it would be promoted to the *current version sublibrary*. This copy was sacrosanct, touched only to fix crippling bugs. It was available for use in integration and testing of all new module versions. A program directory on the 7010 kept track of each version of each module, its status, its whereabouts, and its changes.

Two notions are important here. The first is *control*, the idea of program copies belonging to managers who alone can authorize their change. The second is that of *formal separation* and *progression* from the playpen, to integration, to release.

In my opinion this was one of the best-done things in the OS/360 effort. It is a piece of management technology that seems to have been independently developed on several massive programming projects including those at Bell Labs, ICL, and Cambridge University.[2] It is applicable to documentation as well as to programs. It is an indispensable technology.

Program tools. As new debugging techniques appear, the old ones diminish but do not vanish. Thus one needs dumps, source-file editors, snapshot dumps, even traces.

Likewise one needs a full set of utilities for putting decks on disks, making tape copies, printing files, changing catalogs. If one commissions a project toolmaker early in the process, these can be done once and can be ready by time they are needed.

Documentation system.   Among all tools, the one that saves the most labor may well be a computerized text-editing system, operating on a dependable vehicle. We had a very handy one, devised by J. W. Franklin. Without it I expect OS/360 manuals would have been far later and more cryptic. There are those who would argue that the OS/360 six-foot shelf of manuals represents verbal diarrhea, that the very voluminosity introduces a new kind of incomprehensibility. And there is some truth in that.

But I respond in two ways. First, the OS/360 documentation is overwhelming in bulk, but the reading plan is carefully laid out; if one uses it selectively, he can ignore most of the bulk most of the time. One must consider the OS/360 documentation as a library or an encyclopedia, not a set of mandatory texts.

Second, this is far preferable to the severe underdocumentation that characterizes most programming systems. I will quickly agree, however, that the writing could be vastly improved in some places, and that the result of better writing would be reduced bulk. Some parts (e.g., *Concepts and Facilities*) are very well-written now.

Performance simulator.   Better have one. Build it outside-in, as we will discuss in the next chapter. Use the same top-down design for the performance simulator, the logical simulator, and the product. Start it very early. Listen to it when it speaks.

High-Level Language and Interactive Programming

The most important two tools for system programming today are two that were not used in OS/360 development almost a decade ago. They are still not widely used, but all evidence points to their power and applicability. They are (1) high-level language and (2) interactive programming. I am convinced that only inertia and sloth prevent the universal adoption of these tools; the technical difficulties are no longer valid excuses.

High-level language.   The chief reasons for using a high-level language are productivity and debugging speed. We have discussed productivity earlier (Chapter 8). There is not a lot of numerical evidence, but what there is suggests improvement by integral factors, not just incremental percentages.

The debugging improvement comes from the fact that there are fewer bugs, and they are easier to find. There are fewer because one avoids an entire level of exposure to error, a level on which one makes not only syntactic errors but semantic ones, such as misusing registers. The bugs are easier to find because the compiler diagnostics help find them and, more important, because it is very easy to insert debugging snapshots.

For me, these productivity and debugging reasons are overwhelming. I cannot easily conceive of a programming system I would build in assembly language.

Well, what about the classical objections to such a tool? There are three: It doesn't let me do what I want. The object code is too big. The object code is too slow.

As to function, I believe the objection is no longer valid. All testimony indicates that one can do what he needs to do, but that it takes work to find out how, and one may occasionally need unlovely artifices.[3,4]

As to space, the new optimizing compilers are beginning to be very satisfactory, and this improvement will continue.

As to speed, optimizing compilers now produce some code that is faster than most programmer's handwritten code. Furthermore, one can usually solve speed problems by replacing from one to five percent of a compiler-generated program by handwritten substitute after the former is fully debugged.[5]

What high-level language should one use for system programming? The only reasonable candidate today is PL/I.[6] It has a very full set of functions; it is matched to operating system environments; and a variety of compilers are available, some interactive, some fast, some very diagnostic, and some producing highly optimized code. I myself find it faster to work out algorithms in APL; then I translate these to PL/I for matching to the system environment.

Interactive programming.   One of the justifications for MIT's Multics project was its usefulness for building programming systems. Multics (and following it, IBM's TSS) differs in concept from other interactive computing systems in exactly those respects necessary for systems programming: many levels of sharing and protection for data and programs, extensive library management, and facilities for cooperative work among terminal users. I am convinced that interactive systems will never displace batch systems for many applications. But I think the Multics team has made its most convincing case in the system-programming application.

There is not yet much evidence available on the true fruitfulness of such apparently powerful tools. There *is* a widespread recognition that debugging is the hard and slow part of system programming, and slow turnaround is the bane of debugging. So the logic of interactive programming seems inexorable.[7]

Program	Size	Batch (B) or Conversational (C)	Instructions/man–year
ESS code	800,000	B	500–1000
7094 ESS support	120,000	B	2100–3400
360 ESS support	32,000	C	8000
360 ESS support	8,300	B	4000

Fig. 12.2 Comparative productivity under batch and conversational programming

Further, we hear good testimonies from many who have built little systems or parts of systems in this way. The only numbers I have seen for effects on programming of large systems were reported by John Harr of Bell Labs. They are shown in Fig. 12.2. These numbers are for writing, assembling, and debugging programs. The first program is mostly control program; the other three are language translators, editors, and such. Harr's data suggest that an interactive facility at least doubles productivity in system programming.[8]

The effective use of most interactive tools requires that the work be done in a high-level language, for teletype and typewriter terminals cannot be used to debug by dumping memory. With a high-level language, source can be easily edited and selective printouts easily done. Together they make a pair of sharp tools indeed.

13
The Whole and the Parts

13
The Whole and the Parts

I can call spirits from the vasty deep.

Why so can I, or so can any man; but will they come when you do call for them?

SHAKESPEARE, *KING HENRY* IV, *PART* I

The modern magic, like the old, has its boastful practitioners: "I can write programs that control air traffic, intercept ballistic missiles, reconcile bank accounts, control production lines." To which the answer comes, "So can I, and so can any man, but do they work when you do write them?"

How does one build a program to work? How does one test a program? And how does one integrate a tested set of component programs into a tested and dependable system? We have touched upon the techniques here and there; let us now consider them somewhat more systematically.

Designing the Bugs Out

Bug-proofing the definition.   The most pernicious and subtle bugs are system bugs arising from mismatched assumptions made by the authors of various components. The approach to conceptual integrity discussed above in Chapters 4, 5, and 6 addresses these problems directly. In short, conceptual integrity of the product not only makes it easier to use, it also makes it easier to build and less subject to bugs.

So does the detailed, painstaking architectural effort implied by that approach. V. A. Vyssotsky, of Bell Telephone Laboratories' Safeguard Project, says, "The crucial task is to get the product defined. Many, many failures concern exactly those aspects that were never quite specified."[1] Careful function definition, careful specification, and the disciplined exorcism of frills of function and flights of technique all reduce the number of system bugs that have to be found.

Testing the specification.   Long before any code exists, the specification must be handed to an outside testing group to be scrutinized for completeness and clarity. As Vyssotsky says, the developers themselves cannot do this: "They won't tell you they don't understand it; they will happily invent their way through the gaps and obscurities."

Top-down design.   In a very clear 1971 paper, Niklaus Wirth formalized a design procedure which had been used for years by the best programmers.[2] Furthermore, his notions, although stated for program design, apply completely to the design of complex systems of programs. The division of system building into architecture, implementation, and realization is an embodiment of these notions; furthermore, each of the architecture, implementation, and realization can be best done by top-down methods.

Briefly, Wirth's procedure is to identify design as a sequence of *refinement steps.* One sketches a rough task definition and a rough solution method that achieves the principal result. Then one examines the definition more closely to see how the result differs from what is wanted, and one takes the large steps of the solution and breaks them down into smaller steps. Each refinement in the definition of the task becomes a refinement in the algorithm for solution, and each may be accompanied by a refinement in the data representation.

From this process one identifies *modules* of solution or of data whose further refinement can proceed independently of other work. The degree of this modularity determines the adaptability and changeability of the program.

Wirth advocates using as high-level a notation as is possible at each step, exposing the concepts and concealing the details until further refinement becomes necessary.

A good top-down design avoids bugs in several ways. First, the clarity of structure and representation makes the precise statement of requirements and functions of the modules easier. Second, the partitioning and independence of modules avoids system bugs. Third, the suppression of detail makes flaws in the structure more apparent. Fourth, the design can be tested at each of its refinement steps, so testing can start earlier and focus on the proper level of detail at each step.

The process of step-wise refinement does not mean that one never has to go back, scrap the top level, and start the whole thing again as he encounters some unexpectedly knotty detail. Indeed, that happens often. But it is much easier to see exactly when and why one should throw away a gross design and start over. Many poor systems come from an attempt to salvage a bad basic design and patch it with all kinds of cosmetic relief. Top-down design reduces the temptation.

I am persuaded that top-down design is the most important new programming formalization of the decade.

Structured programming.   Another important set of new ideas for designing the bugs out of programs derives largely from Dijkstra,[3] and is built on a theoretical structure by Böhm and Jacopini.[4]

Basically the approach is to design programs whose control structures consist only of loops defined by a statement such as DO WHILE, and conditional portions delineated into groups of statements marked with brackets and conditioned by an IF . . . THEN . . . ELSE. Böhm and Jacopini show these structures to be theoretically sufficient; Dijkstra argues that the alternative, unrestrained branching via GO TO, produces structures that lend themselves to logical errors.

The basic notion is surely sound. Many criticisms have been made, and additional control structures, such as an n-way branch (the so-called CASE statement) for distinguishing among many contingencies, and a disaster bail-out (GO TO ABNORMAL END) are very convenient. Further, some have become very doctrinaire about avoiding all GO TO's, and that seems excessive.

The important point, and the one vital to constructing bug-free programs, is that one wants to think about the control structures of a system as control structures, not as individual branch statements. This way of thinking is a major step forward.

Component Debugging

The procedures for debugging programs have been through a great cycle in the past twenty years, and in some ways they are back where they started. The cycle has gone through four steps, and it is fun to trace them and see the motivation for each.

On-machine debugging.   Early machines had relatively poor input-output equipment, and long input-output delays. Typically, the machine read and wrote paper tape or magnetic tape and off-line facilities were used for tape preparation and printing. This made tape input-output intolerably awkward for debugging, so the console was used instead. Thus debugging was designed to allow as many trials as possible per machine session.

The programmer carefully designed his debugging procedure —planning where to stop, what memory locations to examine, what to find there, and what to do if he didn't. This meticulous programming of himself as a debugging machine might well take half as long as writing the computer program to be debugged.

The cardinal sin was to push START boldly without having segmented the program into test sections with planned stops.

Memory dumps.   On-machine debugging was very effective. In a two-hour session, one could get perhaps a dozen shots. But computers were very scarce, and very costly, and the thought of all that machine time going to waste was horrifying.

So when high-speed printers were attached on-line, the technique changed. One ran a program until a check failed, and then dumped the whole memory. Then began the laborious desk work, accounting for each memory location's contents. The desk time was not much different than that for on-machine debugging; but it occurred after the test run, in deciphering, rather than before, in planning. Debugging for any particular user took much longer, because test shots depended upon batch turnaround time. The whole procedure, however, was designed to minimize computer time use, and to serve as many programmers as possible.

Snapshots.   The machines on which memory dumping was developed had 2000–4000 words, or 8K to 16K bytes of memory. But memory sizes grew by leaps and bounds, and total memory dumping became impractical. So people developed techniques for selective dumping, selective tracing, and for inserting snapshots into programs. The OS/360 TESTRAN is an end-of-the-line in this direction, allowing one to insert snapshots into a program without reassembly or recompilation.

Interactive debugging. In 1959 Codd and his coworkers[5] and Strachey[6] each reported work aimed at time-shared debugging, a way of achieving both the instant turnaround of on-machine debugging and the efficient machine use of batch debugging. The computer would have multiple programs in memory, ready for execution. A terminal, controlled only by program, would be associated with each program being debugged. Debugging would be under control of a supervisory program. When the programmer at a terminal stopped his program to examine progress or to make changes, the supervisor would run another program, thus keeping the machines busy.

Codd's multiprogramming system was developed, but the emphasis was on throughput enhancement by efficient input-output utilization, and interactive debugging was not implemented. Strachey's ideas were improved and implemented in 1963 in an experimental system for the 7090 by Corbató and colleagues at MIT.[7] This development led to the MULTICS, TSS, and other time-sharing systems of today.

The chief user-perceived differences between on-machine debugging as first practiced and the interactive debugging of today are the facilities made possible by the presence of the supervisory program and its associated language interpreters. One can program and debug in a high-level language. Efficient editing facilities make changes and snapshots easy.

Return to the instant-turnaround capability of on-machine debugging has not yet brought a return to the preplanning of debugging sessions. In a sense such preplanning is not so necessary as before, since machine time doesn't waste away while one sits and thinks.

Nevertheless, Gold's interesting experimental results show that three times as much progress in interactive debugging is made on the first interaction of each session as on subsequent interactions.[8] This strongly suggests that we are not realizing the potential of interaction due to lack of session planning. The time has come to dust off the old on-machine techniques.

I find that proper use of a good terminal system requires two hours at the desk for each two-hour session on the terminal. Half of this time is spent in sweeping up after the last session: updating my debugging log, filing updated program listings in my system notebook, explaining strange phenomena. The other half is spent in preparation: planning changes and improvements and designing detailed tests for next time. Without such planning, it is hard to stay productive for as much as two hours. Without the post-session sweep-up, it is hard to keep the succession of terminal sessions systematic and forward-moving.

Test cases. As for the design of actual debugging procedures and test cases, Gruenberger has an especially good treatment,[9] and there are shorter treatments in other standard texts. [10,11]

System Debugging

The unexpectedly hard part of building a programming system is system test. I have already discussed some of the reasons for both the difficulty and its unexpectedness. From all of that, one should be convinced of two things: system debugging will take longer than one expects, and its difficulty justifies a thoroughly systematic and planned approach. Let us now see what such an approach involves.[12]

Use debugged components. Common sense, if not common practice, dictates that one should begin system debugging only after the pieces seem to work.

Common practice departs from this in two ways. First is the bolt-it-together-and-try approach. This seems to be based on the notion that there will be system (i.e., interface) bugs in addition to the component bugs. The sooner one puts the pieces together, the sooner the system bugs will emerge. Somewhat less sophisticated is the notion that by using the pieces to test each other, one avoids a lot of test scaffolding. Both of these are obviously true, but experience shows that they are not the whole truth—the use of clean, debugged components saves much more time in system testing than that spent on scaffolding and thorough component test.

A little more subtle is the "documented bug" approach. This says that a component is ready to enter system test when all the flaws are *found,* well before the time when all are *fixed.* Then in system testing, so the theory goes, one knows the expected effects of these bugs and can ignore those effects, concentrating on the new phenomena.

All this is just wishful thinking, invented to rationalize away the pain of slipped schedules. One does *not* know all the expected effects of known bugs. If things were straightforward, system testing wouldn't be hard. Furthermore, the fixing of the documented component bugs will surely inject unknown bugs, and then system test is confused.

Build plenty of scaffolding.   By scaffolding I mean all programs and data built for debugging purposes but never intended to be in the final product. It is not unreasonable for there to be half as much code in scaffolding as there is in product.

One form of scaffolding is the *dummy component,* which consists only of interfaces and perhaps some faked data or some small test cases. For example, a system may include a sort program which isn't finished yet. Its neighbors can be tested by using a dummy program that merely reads and tests the format of input data, and spews out a set of well-formatted meaningless but ordered data.

Another form is the *miniature file.* A very common form of system bug is misunderstanding of formats for tape and disk files. So it is worthwhile to build some little files that have only a few typical records, but all the descriptions, pointers, etc.

The limiting case of miniature file is the *dummy file,* which really isn't there at all. OS/360's Job Control Language provides such facility, and it is extremely useful for component debugging.

Yet another form of scaffolding are *auxiliary programs.* Generators for test data, special analysis printouts, cross-reference table analyzers, are all examples of the special-purpose jigs and fixtures one may want to build.[13]

Control changes.   Tight control during test is one of the impressive techniques of hardware debugging, and it applies as well to software systems.

First, somebody must be in charge. He and he alone must authorize component changes or substitution of one version for another.

Then, as discussed above, there must be controlled copies of the system: one locked-up copy of the latest versions, used for component testing; one copy under test, with fixes being installed; playpen copies where each man can work away on his component, doing both fixes and extensions.

In System/360 engineering models, one saw occasional strands of purple wire among the routine yellow wires. When a bug was found, two things were done. A quick fix was devised and installed on the system, so testing could proceed. This change was put on in purple wire, so it stuck out like a sore thumb. It was entered in the log. Meanwhile, an official change document was prepared and started into the design automation mill. Eventually this resulted in updated drawings and wire lists, and a new back panel in which the change was implemented in printed circuitry or yellow wire. Now the physical model and the paper were together again, and the purple wire was gone.

Programming needs a purple-wire technique, and it badly needs tight control and deep respect for the paper that ultimately is the product. The vital ingredients of such technique are the logging of all changes in a journal and the distinction, carried conspicuously in source code, between quick patches and thought-through, tested, documented fixes.

Add one component at a time.   This precept, too, is obvious, but optimism and laziness tempt us to violate it. To do it requires dummies and other scaffolding, and that takes work. And after all, perhaps all that work won't be needed? Perhaps there are no bugs?

No! Resist the temptation! That is what systematic system testing is all about. One must assume that there will be lots of bugs, and plan an orderly procedure for snaking them out.

Note that one must have thorough test cases, testing the partial systems after each new piece is added. And the old ones, run successfully on the last partial sum, must be rerun on the new one to test for system regression.

Quantize updates.   As the system comes up, the component builders will from time to time appear, bearing hot new versions of their pieces—faster,smaller, more complete, or putatively less buggy. The replacement of a working component by a new version requires the same systematic testing procedure that adding a new component does, although it should require less time, for more complete and efficient test cases will usually be available.

Each team building another component has been using the most recent tested version of the integrated system as a test bed for debugging its piece. Their work will be set back by having that test bed change under them. Of course it must. But the changes need to be quantized. Then each user has periods of productive stability, interrupted by bursts of test-bed change. This seems to be much less disruptive than a constant rippling and trembling.

Lehman and Belady offer evidence that quanta should be very large and widely spaced or else very small and frequent.[14] The latter strategy is more subject to instability, according to their model. My experience confirms it: I would never risk that strategy in practice.

Quantized changes neatly accommodate a purple-wire technique. The quick patch holds until the next regular release of the component, which should incorporate the fix in tested and documented form.

14
Hatching a Catastrophe

14
Hatching a Catastrophe

None love the bearer of bad news.

SOPHOCLES

How does a project get to be a year late?
. . . One day at a time.

A. Canova, "Ercole e Lica," 1802. Hercules hurls to his death the messenger Lycas, who innocently brought the death-garment.

Scala/Art Resource, NY

When one hears of disastrous schedule slippage in a project, he imagines that a series of major calamities must have befallen it. Usually, however, the disaster is due to termites, not tornadoes; and the schedule has slipped imperceptibly but inexorably. Indeed, major calamities are easier to handle; one responds with major force, radical reorganization, the invention of new approaches. The whole team rises to the occasion.

But the day-by-day slippage is harder to recognize, harder to prevent, harder to make up. Yesterday a key man was sick, and a meeting couldn't be held. Today the machines are all down, because lightning struck the building's power transformer. Tomorrow the disk routines won't start testing, because the first disk is a week late from the factory. Snow, jury duty, family problems, emergency meetings with customers, executive audits—the list goes on and on. Each one only postpones some activity by a half-day or a day. And the schedule slips, one day at a time.

Milestones or Millstones?

How does one control a big project on a tight schedule? The first step is to *have* a schedule. Each of a list of events, called milestones, has a date. Picking the dates is an estimating problem, discussed already and crucially dependent on experience.

For picking the milestones there is only one relevant rule. Milestones must be concrete, specific, measurable events, defined with knife-edge sharpness. Coding, for a counterexample, is "90 percent finished" for half of the total coding time. Debugging is "99 percent complete" most of the time. "Planning complete" is an event one can proclaim almost at will.[1]

Concrete milestones, on the other hand, are 100-percent events. "Specifications signed by architects and implementers," "source coding 100 percent complete, keypunched, entered into disk library," "debugged version passes all test cases." These concrete milestones demark the vague phases of planning, coding, debugging.

It is more important that milestones be sharp-edged and un-ambiguous than that they be easily verifiable by the boss. Rarely will a man lie about milestone progress, *if* the milestone is so sharp that he can't deceive himself. But if the milestone is fuzzy, the boss often understands a different report from that which the man gives. To supplement Sophocles, no one enjoys bearing bad news, either, so it gets softened without any real intent to deceive.

Two interesting studies of estimating behavior by government contractors on large-scale development projects show that:

1. Estimates of the length of an activity, made and revised carefully every two weeks before the activity starts, do not significantly change as the start time draws near, no matter how wrong they ultimately turn out to be.
2. *During* the activity, *over*estimates of duration come steadily down as the activity proceeds.
3. *Underestimates* do not change significantly during the activity until about three weeks before the scheduled completion.[2]

Sharp milestones are in fact a service to the team, and one they can properly expect from a manager. The fuzzy milestone is the harder burden to live with. It is in fact a millstone that grinds down morale, for it deceives one about lost time until it is irremediable. And chronic schedule slippage is a morale-killer.

"The Other Piece Is Late, Anyway"

A schedule slips a day; so what? Who gets excited about a one-day slip? We can make it up later. And the other piece into which ours fits is late, anyway.

A baseball manager recognizes a nonphysical talent, *hustle,* as an essential gift of great players and great teams. It is the characteristic of running faster than necessary, moving sooner than necessary, trying harder than necessary. It is essential for great programming teams, too. Hustle provides the cushion, the reserve capacity, that enables a team to cope with routine mishaps, to anticipate and forfend minor calamities. The calculated response, the measured effort, are the wet blankets that dampen hustle. As we have seen, one *must* get excited about a one-day slip. Such are the elements of catastrophe.

But not all one-day slips are equally disastrous. So some calculation of response is necessary, though hustle be dampened. How does one tell which slips matter? There is no substitute for a PERT chart or a critical-path schedule. Such a network shows who waits for what. It shows who is on the critical path, where any slip moves the end date. It also shows how much an activity can slip before it moves into the critical path.

The PERT technique, strictly speaking, is an elaboration of critical-path scheduling in which one estimates three times for every event, times corresponding to different probabilities of meeting the estimated dates. I do not find this refinement to be worth the extra effort, but for brevity I will call any critical path network a PERT chart.

The preparation of a PERT chart is the most valuable part of its use. Laying out the network, identifying the dependencies, and estimating the legs all force a great deal of very specific planning very early in a project. The first chart is always terrible, and one invents and invents in making the second one.

As the project proceeds, the PERT chart provides the answer to the demoralizing excuse, "The other piece is late anyhow." It shows how hustle is needed to keep one's own part off the critical path, and it suggests ways to make up the lost time in the other part.

Under the Rug

When a first-line manager sees his small team slipping behind, he is rarely inclined to run to the boss with this woe. The team might be able to make it up, or he should be able to invent or reorganize to solve the problem. Then why worry the boss with it? So far, so good. Solving such problems is exactly what the first-line manager is there for. And the boss does have enough real worries demanding his action that he doesn't seek others. So all the dirt gets swept under the rug.

But every boss needs two kinds of information, exceptions to plan that require action and a status picture for education.[3] For that purpose he needs to know the status of all his teams. Getting a true picture of that status is hard.

The first-line manager's interests and those of the boss have an inherent conflict here. The first-line manager fears that if he reports his problem, the boss will act on it. Then his action will preempt the manager's function, diminish his authority, foul up his other plans. So as long as the manager thinks he can solve it alone, he doesn't tell the boss.

Two rug-lifting techniques are open to the boss. Both must be used. The first is to reduce the role conflict and inspire sharing of status. The other is to yank the rug back.

Reducing the role conflict. The boss must first distinguish between action information and status information. He must discipline himself *not* to act on problems his managers can solve, and *never* to act on problems when he is explicitly reviewing status. I once knew a boss who invariably picked up the phone to give orders before the end of the first paragraph in a status report. That response is guaranteed to squelch full disclosure.

Conversely, when the manager knows his boss will accept status reports without panic or preemption, he comes to give honest appraisals.

This whole process is helped if the boss labels meetings, reviews, conferences, as *status-review* meetings versus *problem-action* meetings, and controls himself accordingly. Obviously one may call a problem-action meeting as a consequence of a status meeting, if he believes a problem is out of hand. But at least everybody knows what the score is, and the boss thinks twice before grabbing the ball.

Yanking the rug off.   Nevertheless, it is necessary to have review techniques by which the true status is made known, whether cooperatively or not. The PERT chart with its frequent sharp milestones is the basis for such review. On a large project one may want to review some part of it each week, making the rounds once a month or so.

A report showing milestones and actual completions is the key document. Figure 14.1 shows an excerpt from such a report. This report shows some troubles. Specifications approval is overdue on several components. Manual (SLR) approval is overdue on another, and one is late getting out of the first state (Alpha) of the independently conducted product test. So such a report serves as an agenda for the meeting of 1 February. Everyone knows the questions, and the component manager should be prepared to explain why it's late, when it will be finished, what steps he's taking, and what help, if any, he needs from the boss or collateral groups.

V. Vyssotsky of Bell Telephone Laboratories adds the following observation:

I have found it handy to carry both "scheduled" and "estimated" dates in the milestone report. The scheduled dates are the property of the project manager and represent a consistent work plan for the project as a whole, and one which is a priori a reasonable plan. The estimated dates are the property of the lowest level manager who has cognizance over the piece of work in question, and represents his best judgment as to when it will actually happen, given the resources he has available and when he received (or has commitments for delivery of) his prerequisite inputs. The project manager has to keep his fingers off the estimated dates, and put the emphasis on getting accurate, unbiased estimates rather than palatable optimistic estimates or self-protective conservative ones. Once this is clearly established in every-one's mind, the project manager can see quite a ways into the future where he is going to be in trouble if he doesn't do something. [4]

OS/360 SYSTEM/360 SUMMARY STATUS REPORT
LANGUAGE PROCESSORS + SERVICE PROGRAMS
AS OF FEBRUARY 01.1965

A=APPROVAL C=COMPLETED
*=REVISED PLANNED DATE NE=NOT ESTABLISHED

PROJECT	LOCATION	COMMITMNT ANNOUNCE RELEASE	OBJECTIVE AVAILABLE APPROVED	SPECS AVAILABLE APPROVED	SRL AVAILABLE APPROVED	ALPHA TEST ENTRY EXIT	COMP TEST START COMPLETE	SYS TEST START COMPLETE	BULLETIN AVAILABLE APPROVED	BETA TEST ENTRY EXIT
OPERATING SYSTEM										
12K DESIGN LEVEL (E)										
ASSEMBLY	SAN JOSE	04/--/4 C 12/31/5	10/28/4 C	10/13/4 C 01/11/5	11/13/4 C 11/18/4 A	01/15/5 02/22/5 C				09/01/5 11/30/5
FORTRAN	POK	04/--/4 C 12/31/5	10/28/4 C	10/21/4 C 01/22/5	12/17/4 C 12/19/4 A	01/15/5 02/22/5 C				09/01/5 11/30/5
COBOL	ENDICOTT	04/--/4 C 12/31/5	10/28/4 C	10/15/4 C 01/20/5 A	11/17/4 C 12/08/4 A	01/15/5 02/22/5 C				09/01/5 11/30/5
RPG	SAN JOSE	04/--/4 C 12/31/5	10/28/4 C	09/30/4 C 01/05/5 A	12/02/4 C 01/18/5 A	01/15/5 02/22/5 C				09/01/5 11/30/5
UTILITIES	TIME/LIFE	04/--/4 C 12/31/5	06/24/4 C		11/20/4 C 11/30/4 A					09/01/5 11/30/5
SORT 1	POK	04/--/4 C 12/31/5	10/28/4 C	10/19/4 C 01/11/5	11/12/4 C 11/30/4 A	01/15/5 03/22/5 C				09/01/5 11/30/5
SORT 2	POK	04/--/4 C 06/30/6	10/28/4 C	10/19/4 C 01/11/5	11/12/4 C 11/30/4 A	01/15/5 03/22/5 C				03/01/6 05/30/6
44K DESIGN LEVEL (F)										
ASSEMBLY	SAN JOSE	04/--/4 C 12/31/5	10/28/4 C	10/13/4 C 01/11/5	11/13/4 C 11/18/4 A	02/15/5 03/22/5				09/01/5 11/30/5
COBOL	TIME/LIFE	04/--/4 C 06/30/6	10/28/4 C	10/15/4 C 01/20/5 A	11/17/4 C 12/08/4 A	02/15/5 03/22/5				03/01/6 05/30/6
NPL	HURSLEY	04/--/4 C 03/31/6	10/28/4 C							
2250	KINGSTON	03/30/4 C 03/31/6	11/05/4 C	12/08/4 C 01/04/5	01/13/5 C 01/29/5	01/04/5 01/29/5 C				01/03/6 NE
2280	KINGSTON	06/30/4 C 09/30/6	11/05/4 C			04/01/5 04/30/5				01/28/6 NE
200K DESIGN LEVEL (H)										
ASSEMBLY	TIME/LIFE		10/28/4 C							
FORTRAN	POK	04/--/4 C 06/30/6	10/28/4 C	10/16/4 C 01/11/5	11/11/4 C 12/10/4 A	02/15/5 03/22/5				03/01/6 05/30/6
NPL	HURSLEY	04/--/4 C 03/31/7	10/28/4 C			07/--/5				01/--/7
NPL H	POK	04/--/4 C	03/30/4 C			02/01/5 04/01/5				10/15/5 12/15/5

Figure 14.1

The preparation of the PERT chart is a function of the boss and the managers reporting to him. Its updating, revision, and reporting requires the attention of a small (one to three man) staff group which serves as an extension of the boss. Such a *Plans and Controls* team is invaluable for a large project. It has no authority except to ask all the line managers when they will have set or changed milestones, and whether milestones have been met. Since the Plans and Controls group handles all the paperwork, the burden on the line managers is reduced to the essentials—making the decisions.

We had a skilled, enthusiastic, and diplomatic Plans and Controls group, run by A. M. Pietrasanta, who devoted considerable inventive talent to devising effective but unobtrusive control methods. As a result, I found his group to be widely respected and more than tolerated. For a group whose role is inherently that of an irritant, this is quite an accomplishment.

The investment of a modest amount of skilled effort in a Plans and Controls function is very rewarding. It makes far more difference in project accomplishment than if these people worked directly on building the product programs. For the Plans and Controls group is the watchdog who renders the imperceptible delays visible and who points up the critical elements. It is the early warning system against losing a year, one day at a time.

15
The Other Face

15
The Other Face

A reconstruction of Stonehenge, the world's largest undocumented computer.
The Bettman Archive

A computer program is a message from a man to a machine. The rigidly marshaled syntax and the scrupulous definitions all exist to make intention clear to the dumb engine.

But a written program has another face, that which tells its story to the human user. For even the most private of programs, some such communication is necessary; memory will fail the author-user, and he will require refreshing on the details of his handiwork.

How much more vital is the documentation for a public program, whose user is remote from the author in both time and space! For the program product, the other face to the user is fully as important as the face to the machine.

Most of us have quietly excoriated the remote and anonymous author of some skimpily documented program. And many of us have therefore tried to instill in new programmers an attitude about documentation that would inspire for a lifetime, overcoming sloth and schedule pressure. By and large we have failed. I think we have used wrong methods.

Thomas J. Watson, Sr. told the story of his first experience as a cash register salesman in upstate New York. Charged with enthusiasm, he sallied out with his wagon loaded with cash registers. He worked his territory diligently but without selling a one. Downcast, he reported to his boss. The sales manager listened a while, then said, "Help me load some registers into the wagon, harness the horse, and let's go again." They did, and the two called on customer after customer, with the older man *showing how* to sell cash registers. All evidence indicates that the lesson took.

For several years I diligently lectured my software engineering class on the necessity and propriety of good documentation, exhorting them ever more fervently and eloquently. It didn't work. I assumed they had learned how to document properly and were failing from lack of zeal. Then I tried loading some cash registers into the wagon; i.e., *showing* them how the job is done. This has been much more successful. So the remainder of this essay will downplay exhortation and concentrate on the "how" of good documentation.

What Documentation Is Required?

Different levels of documentation are required for the casual user of a program, for the user who must depend upon a program, and for the user who must adapt a program for changes in circumstance or purpose.

To use a program.   Every user needs a prose description of the program. Most documentation fails in giving too little overview. The trees are described, the bark and leaves are commented, but there is no map of the forest. To write a useful prose description, stand way back and come in slowly:

1. *Purpose.* What is the main function, the reason for the program?
2. *Environment.* On what machines, hardware configurations, and operating system configurations will it run?
3. *Domain and range.* What domain of input is valid? What range of output can legitimately appear?
4. *Functions realized and algorithms used.* Precisely what does it do?
5. *Input-output formats,.* precise and complete.
6. *Operating instructions,* including normal and abnormal ending behavior, as seen at the console and on the outputs.
7. *Options.* What choices does the user have about functions? Exactly how are those choices specified?
8. *Running time.* How long does it take to do a problem of specified size on a specified configuration?
9. *Accuracy and checking.* How precise are the answers expected to be? What means of checking accuracy are incorporated?

Often all this information can be set forth in three or four pages. That requires close attention to conciseness and precision. Most of this document needs to be drafted before the program is written, for it embodies basic planning decisions.

To believe a program.   The description of how it is used must be supplemented with some description of how one knows it is working. This means test cases.

Every copy of a program shipped should include some small test cases that can be routinely used to reassure the user that he has a faithful copy, accurately loaded into the machine.

Then one needs more thorough test cases, which are normally run only after a program is modified. These fall into three parts of the input data domain:

1. Mainline cases that test the program's chief functions for commonly encountered data.
2. Barely legitimate cases that probe the edge of the input data domain, ensuring that largest possible values, smallest possible values, and all kinds of valid exceptions work.
3. Barely illegitimate cases that probe the domain boundary from the other side, ensuring that invalid inputs raise proper diagnostic messages.

To modify a program.   Adapting a program or fixing it requires considerably more information. Of course the full detail is required, and that is contained in a well-commented listing. For the modifier, as well as the more casual user, the crying need is for a clear, sharp overview, this time of the internal structure. What are the components of such an overview?

1. A flow chart or subprogram structure graph. More on this later.
2. Complete descriptions of the algorithms used, or else references to such descriptions in the literature.
3. An explanation of the layout of all files used.
4. An overview of the pass structure—the sequence in which data or programs are brought from tape or disk—and what is accomplished on each pass.
5. A discussion of modifications contemplated in the original design, the nature and location of hooks and exits, and discursive discussion of the ideas of the original author about what modifications might be desirable and how one might proceed. His observations on hidden pitfalls are also useful.

The Flow-Chart Curse

The flow chart is a most thoroughly oversold piece of program documentation. Many programs don't need flow charts at all; few programs need more than a one-page flow chart.

Flow charts show the decision structure of a program, which is only one aspect of its structure. They show decision structure rather elegantly when the flow chart is on one page, but the over-

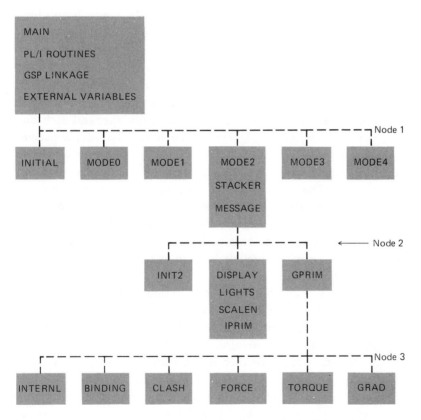

Fig. 15.1 A program structure graph. (Courtesy of W. V. Wright)

view breaks down badly when one has multiple pages, sewed together with numbered exits and connectors.

The one-page flow chart for a substantial program becomes essentially a diagram of program structure, and of phases or steps. As such it is very handy. Figure 15.1 shows such a subprogram structure graph.

Of course such a structure graph neither follows nor needs the painfully wrought ANSI flow-charting standards. All the rules on box shapes, connectors, numbering, etc. are needed only to give intelligibility to detailed flow charts.

The detailed blow-by-blow flow chart, however, is an obsolete nuisance, suitable only for initiating beginners into algorithmic thinking. When introduced by Goldstine and von Neumann,[1] the little boxes and their contents served as a high-level language, grouping the inscrutable machine-language statements into clusters of significance. As Iverson early recognized,[2] in a systematic high-level language the clustering is already done, and each box contains a statement (Fig. 15.2). Then the boxes themselves become no more than a tedious and space-hogging exercise in drafting; they might as well be eliminated. Then nothing is left but the arrows. The arrows joining a statement to its successor are redundant; erase them. That leaves only GO TO's. And if one follows good practice and uses block structure to minimize GO TO's, there aren't many arrows, but they aid comprehension immensely. One might as well draw them on the listing and eliminate the flow chart altogether.

In fact, flow charting is more preached than practiced. I have never seen an experienced programmer who routinely made detailed flow charts before beginning to write programs. Where organization standards require flow charts, these are almost invariably done after the fact. Many shops proudly use machine programs to generate this "indispensable design tool" from the completed code. I think this universal experience is not an embarrassing and deplorable departure from good practice, to be acknowledged only with a nervous laugh. Instead it is the application of good judgment, and it teaches us something about the utility of flow charts.

The Apostle Peter said of new Gentile converts and the Jewish law, "Why lay a load on [their] backs which neither our ancestors nor we ourselves were able to carry?" (Acts 15:10, TEV). I would say the same about new programmers and the obsolete practice of flow charting.

Self-Documenting Programs

A basic principle of data processing teaches the folly of trying to maintain independent files in synchronism. It is far better to combine them into one file with each record containing all the information both files held concerning a given key.

Yet our practice in programming documentation violates our own teaching. We typically attempt to maintain a machine-readable form of a program and an independent set of human-readable documentation, consisting of prose and flow charts.

The results in fact confirm our teachings about the folly of separate files. Program documentation is notoriously poor, and its maintenance is worse. Changes made in the program do not promptly, accurately, and invariably appear in the paper.

The solution, I think, is to merge the files, to incorporate the documentation in the source program. This is at once a powerful incentive toward proper maintenance, and an insurance that the documentation will always be handy to the program user. Such programs are called *self-documenting.*

Now clearly this is awkward (but not impossible) if flow charts are to be included. But grant the obsolescence of flow charts and the dominant use of high-level language, and it becomes reasonable to combine the program and the documentation.

The use of a source program as a documentation medium imposes some constraints. On the other hand, the intimate availability of the source program, line by line, to the reader of the documentation makes possible new techniques. The time has

```
PGM4: PROCEDURE OPTIONS (MAIN);

      DECLARE SALEFL FILE
          RECORD
          INPUT
          ENVIRONMENT (F(80) MEDIUM (SYSIPT, 2501)) ;
      DECLARE PRINT4 FILE
          RECORD
          OUTPUT
          ENVIRONMENT (F(132) MEDIUM (SYSLST,1403) CTLASA);
      DECLARE 01 SALESCARD,
          03 BLANK1         CHARACTER (9),
          03 SALESNUM       PICTURE '9999',
          03 NAME           CHARACTER (25),
          03 BLANK2         CHARACTER (7),
          03 CURRENT_SALES  PICTURE '9999V99',
          03 BLANK3         CHARACTER (29);
      DECLARE 01 SALESLIST,
          03 CONTROL        CHARACTER (1) INITIAL (' '),
          03 SALESNUM_OUT   PICTURE 'ZZZ9',
          03 FILLER1        CHARACTER (5) INITIAL (' '),
          03 NAME_OUT       CHARACTER (25),
          03 FILLER2        CHARACTER (5) INITIAL (' '),
          03 CURRENT_OUT    PICTURE 'Z,ZZZV.99',
          03 FILLER3        CHARACTER (5) INITIAL (' '),
          03 PERCENT        PICTURE 'Z9',
          03 SIGN           CHARACTER (1) INITIAL ('%'),
          03 FILLER4        CHARACTER (5) INITIAL (' '),
          03 COMMISSION     PICTURE 'Z,ZZZV.99',
          03 FILLER5        CHARACTER (63) INITIAL (' ');

      OPEN FILE (SALEFL),FILE (PRINT4);

      ON ENDFILE (SALEFL) GO TO ENDOFJOB;
```

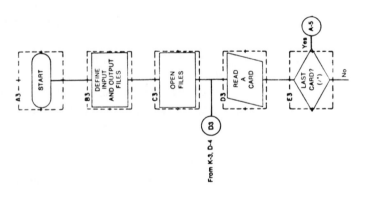

```
READ_CARD:
    READ FILE (SALEFL) INTO (SALESCARD);
    IF CURRENT_SALES < 1000.00 THEN GO TO UNDER_QUOTA
    SALESNUM_OUT=SALESNUM;
    NAME_OUT=NAME;
    CURRENT_OUT=CURRENT_SALES;
    PERCENT=5;
    COMMISSION=CURRENT_SALES*.05;
    WRITE FILE (PRINT4) FROM (SALESLIST);
    GO TO READ_CARD;
```

Fig. 15.2   Comparison of a flow chart and a corresponding PL/I program.
[Abridged and adapted from Figs. 15–41, 15–44, in *Data Processing and Computer Programming: A Modular Approach* by Thomas J. Cashman and William J. Keys (Harper & Row, 1971).]

come to devise radically new approaches and methods for program documentation.

As a principal objective, we must attempt to minimize the burden of documentation, the burden neither we nor our predecessors have been able to bear successfully.

An approach.   The first notion is to use the parts of the program that have to be there anyway, for programming language reasons, to carry as much of the documentation as possible. So labels, declaration statements, and symbolic names are all harnessed to the task of conveying as much meaning as possible to the reader.

A second notion is to use space and format as much as possible to improve readability and show subordination and nesting.

The third notion is to insert the necessary prose documentation into the program as paragraphs of comment. Most programs tend to have enough line-by-line comments; those programs produced to meet stiff organizational standards for "good documentation" often have too many. Even these programs, however, are usually deficient in the paragraph comments that really give intelligibility and overview to the whole thing.

Since the documentation is built into the structure, naming, and formats of the program, much of it *must* be done when the program is first written. But that is when it *should* be written. Since the self-documentation approach minimizes extra work, there are fewer obstacles to doing it then.

Some techniques.   Figure 15.3 shows a self-documenting PL/I program.[3] The numbers in the circles are not part of it; they are meta-documentation keyed to the discussion.

1. Use a separate job name for each run, and maintain a run log showing what was tried, when, and the results. If the name is composed of a mnemonic part (here *QLT*) and a numerical suffix (here *4*), the suffix can be used as a run number, tying listings and log together. This technique requires a new job card for each run, but they can be made up in batches, duplicating the common information.

Fig. 15.3 A self-documenting program. ⟶

```
①  //QLT4 JOB ...

②  QLTSRT7: PROCEDURE (V);

   /**********************************************************************/
③  /*A SORT SUBROUTINE FOR 2500 6-BYTE FIELDS, PASSED AS THE VECTOR V.  A  */
   /*SEPARATELY COMPILED, NOT-MAIN PROCEDURE, WHICH MUST USE AUTOMATIC CORE */
   /*ALLOCATION.                                                          */
   /*                                                                     */
④  /*THE SORT ALGORITHM FOLLOWS BROOKS AND IVERSON, AUTOMATIC DATA PROCESSING,*/
   /*PROGRAM 7.23, P. 350.  THAT ALGORITHM IS REVISED AS FOLLOWS:         */
⑤  /*  STEPS 2-12 ARE SIMPLIFIED FOR M=2.                                 */
   /*  STEP 18 IS EXPANDED TO HANDLE EXPLICIT INDEXING OF THE OUTPUT VECTOR. */
   /*  THE WHOLE FIELD IS USED AS THE SORT KEY.                           */
   /*  MINUS INFINITY IS REPRESENTED BY ZEROS.                            */
   /*  PLUS INFINITY IS REPRESENTED BY ONES.                              */
   /*  THE STATEMENT NUMBERS IN PROG. 7.23 ARE REFLECTED IN THE STATEMENT  */
   /*    LABELS OF THIS PROGRAM.                                          */
   /*  AN IF-THEN-ELSE CONSTRUCTION REQUIRES REPETITION OF A FEW LINES.    */
   /*                                                                     */
   /*TO CHANGE THE DIMENSION OF THE VECTOR TO BE SORTED, ALWAYS CHANGE THE  */
   /*INITIALIZATION OF T.  IF THE SIZE EXCEEDS 4096, CHANGE THE SIZE OF T,TOO.*/
   /*A MORE GENERAL VERSION WOULD PARAMETERIZE THE DIMENSION OF V.         */
   /*                                                                     */
   /*THE PASSED INPUT VECTOR IS REPLACED BY THE REORDERED OUTPUT VECTOR.   */
   /**********************************************************************/

⑥ /* LEGEND  (ZERO-ORIGIN INDEXING)                                      */

   DECLARE
     (H,                   /*INDEX FOR INITIALIZING T                     */
      I,                   /*INDEX OF ITEM TO BE REPLACED                 */
      J,                   /*INITIAL INDEX OF BRANCHES FROM NODE I        */
      K) BINARY FIXED,     /*INDEX IN OUTPUT VECTOR                       */

     (MINF,                /*MINUS INFINITY                               */
      PINF) BIT (48),      /*PLUS INFINITY                                */

      V (*)   BIT (*),     /*PASSED VECTOR TO BE SORTED AND RETURNED      */

      T (0:8190) BIT (48); /*WORKSPACE CONSISTING OF VECTOR TO BE SORTED, FILLED*/
                           /*OUT WITH INFINITIES, PRECEDED BY LOWER LEVELS */
                           /*FILLED UP WITH MINUS INFINITIES              */

   /* NOW INITIALIZATION TO FILL DUMMY LEVELS, TOP LEVEL, AND UNUSED PART OF TOP*/
   /* LEVEL AS REQUIRED.                                                  */

⑦  INIT: MINF= (48) '0'B;
         PINF= (48) '1'B;

         DO L=    0 TO 4094;  T(L) = MINF;       END;
         DO L=    0 TO 2499;  T(L+4095) = V(L);  END;
         DO L=6595 TO 8190;  T(L) = PINF;        END;

⑧  K0:   K = -1;                                                    ⑩
    K1:   I = 0;                 /*                ⑪              <------|  */
    K3:   J = 2*I+1;             /*SET J TO SCAN BRANCHES FROM NODE I.  <-----||  */
    K7:   IF T(J) <= T(J+1)      /*PICK SMALLER BRANCH                 __>__||  */
            THEN                 /*                                        |||  */
         ⑨ DO;           ⑫       /*                                        |||  */
    K11:      T(I) = T(J);       /*REPLACE                                 |||  */
    K13:      IF T(I) = PINF THEN GO TO K16; /*IF INFINITY, REPLACEMENT_+∞_|||  */
                                 /* IS FINISHED                            |||  */
    K12:      I = J;             /*SET INDEX FOR HIGHER LEVEL              ||||  */
            END;                 /*                                        ||||  */
            ELSE                 /*                                     <---+-||  */
            DO;                  /*                                        | ||  */
    K11A:      T(I) = T(J+1);  /*                                          | ||  */
    K13A:      IF T(I) = PINF THEN GO TO K16;    /*                    _+∞_| ||  */
    K12A:      I = J+1;        /*                                        | ||  */
            END;               /*                                     <_ | ||  */
    K14:  IF 2*I < 8191 THEN GO TO K3;  /*GO BACK IF NOT ON TOP LEVEL  ----+-||  */
    K15:  T(I) = PINF;          /*IF TOP LEVEL, FILL WITH INFINITY        |  |  */
    K16:  IF T(0) = PINF THEN RETURN;  /*TEST END OF SORT           <---| |  */
    K17:  IF T(0) = MINF THEN GO TO K1;  /*FLUSH OUT INITIAL DUMMIES  _-∞___|  */
    K18:  K = K+1;                      /*STEP STORAGE INDEX             |  */
          V(K) = T(0);  GO TO K1; ⑫     /*STORE OUTPUT ITEM         -------|  */
   END QLTSRT7;
```

2. Use a program name that is mnemonic but also contains a version identifier. That is, assume there will be several versions. Here the index is the low order digit of the year 1967.

3. Incorporate the prose description as comments to PROCEDURE.

4. Refer to standard literature to document basic algorithms wherever possible. This saves space, usually points to a much fuller treatment than one would provide, and allows the knowledgeable reader to skip it with confidence that he understands you.

5. Show the relationship to the book algorithm:
   a) changes   b) specialization   c) representation

6. Declare all variables. Use mnemonic names. Use comments to convert DECLARE into a complete legend. Note that it already contains names and structural descriptions, it needs only to be augmented with descriptions of *purpose*. By doing so here, one can avoid repeating the names and structural descriptions in a separate treatment.

7. Mark the initialization by a label.

8. Label statements in groups to show correspondences to the statements in the algorithm description in the literature.

9. Use indenting to show structure and grouping.

10. Add logical flow arrows to the listing by hand. They are very helpful in debugging and changing. They may be incorporated in the right margin of the comments space, and made part of the machine-readable text.

11. Use line comments or remark anything that is not obvious. If the techniques above have been used, these will be short and fewer in number than is customary.

12. Put multiple statements on one line, or one statement on several lines to match thought-grouping and to show correspondence to other algorithm description.

Why not?   What are the drawbacks of such an approach to documentation? There are several, which have been real but are becoming imaginary with changing times.

The most serious objection is the increase in the size of the source code that must be stored. As the discipline moves more and more toward on-line storage of source code, this has become a growing consideration. I find myself being briefer in comments to an APL program, which will live on a disk, than on a PL/I one that I will store as cards.

Yet simultaneously we are moving also toward on-line storage of prose documents for access and for updating via computerized text-editing. As shown above, amalgamating prose and program *reduces* the total number of characters to be stored.

A similar answer applies to the argument that self-documenting programs require more keystrokes. A typed document requires at least one keystroke per character per draft. A self-documenting program has fewer total characters and also fewer strokes per character, since drafts aren't retyped.

How about flow charts and structure graphs? If one uses only a highest-level structure graph, it might safely be kept as a separate document, for it is not subject to frequent change. But it can certainly be incorporated into the source program as a comment, and that seems wise.

To what extent are the techniques used above applicable to assembly language programs? I think the basic approach of self-documentation is thoroughly applicable. Space and formats are less free, and thus cannot be so flexibly used. Names and structural declarations can surely be exploited. Macros can help a great deal. The extensive use of paragraph comments is good practice in any language.

But the self-documentation approach is stimulated by the use of high-level languages and finds its greatest power and its greatest justification in high-level languages used with on-line systems, whether batch or interactive. As I have argued, such languages and systems help programmers in very powerful ways. Since machines are made for people, not people for machines, their use makes every form of sense, economic and human.

16

No Silver Bullet—
Essence and Accident
in Software Engineering

16
No Silver Bullet— Essence and Accident in Software Engineering

There is no single development, in either technology or management technique, which by itself promises even one order-of-magnitude improvement within a decade in productivity, in reliability, in simplicity.

The Werewolf of Eschenbach, Germany: line engraving, 1685. Courtesy of The Grainger Collection, New York.

Abstract[1]

All software construction involves essential tasks, the fashioning of the complex conceptual structures that compose the abstract software entity, and accidental tasks, the representation of these abstract entities in programming languages and the mapping of these onto machine languages within space and speed constraints. Most of the big past gains in software productivity have come from removing artificial barriers that have made the accidental tasks inordinately hard, such as severe hardware constraints, awkward programming languages, lack of machine time. How much of what software engineers now do is still devoted to the accidental, as opposed to the essential? Unless it is more than 9/10 of all effort, shrinking all the accidental activities to zero time will not give an order of magnitude improvement.

Therefore it appears that the time has come to address the essential parts of the software task, those concerned with fashioning abstract conceptual structures of great complexity. I suggest:

- Exploiting the mass market to avoid constructing what can be bought.
- Using rapid prototyping as part of a planned iteration in establishing software requirements.
- Growing software organically, adding more and more function to systems as they are run, used, and tested.
- Identifying and developing the great conceptual designers of the rising generation.

Introduction

Of all the monsters who fill the nightmares of our folklore, none terrify more than werewolves, because they transform unexpectedly from the familiar into horrors. For these, we seek bullets of silver that can magically lay them to rest.

The familiar software project has something of this character (at least as seen by the nontechnical manager), usually innocent and straightforward, but capable of becoming a monster of missed schedules, blown budgets, and flawed products. So we hear desperate cries for a silver bullet, something to make software costs drop as rapidly as computer hardware costs do.

But, as we look to the horizon of a decade hence, we see no silver bullet. There is no single development, in either technology or management technique, which by itself promises even one order of magnitude improvement in productivity, in reliability, in simplicity. In this chapter we shall try to see why, by examining both the nature of the software problem and the properties of the bullets proposed.

Skepticism is not pessimism, however. Although we see no startling breakthroughs, and indeed, believe such to be inconsistent with the nature of software, many encouraging innovations are under way. A disciplined, consistent effort to develop, propagate, and exploit them should indeed yield an order-of-magnitude improvement. There is no royal road, but there is a road.

The first step toward the management of disease was replacement of demon theories and humours theories by the germ theory. That very step, the beginning of hope, in itself dashed all hopes of magical solutions. It told workers that progress would be made stepwise, at great effort, and that a persistent, unremitting care would have to be paid to a discipline of cleanliness. So it is with software engineering today.

Does It Have to Be Hard?—Essential Difficulties

Not only are there no silver bullets now in view, the very nature of software makes it unlikely that there will be any—no inventions that will do for software productivity, reliability, and simplicity what electronics, transistors, and large-scale integration did for computer hardware. We cannot expect ever to see twofold gains every two years.

First, we must observe that the anomaly is not that software progress is so slow but that computer hardware progress is so fast. No other technology since civilization began has seen six orders of magnitude price-performance gain in 30 years. In no other technology can one choose to take the gain in *either* improved performance *or* in reduced costs. These gains flow from the transformation of computer manufacture from an assembly industry into a process industry.

Second, to see what rate of progress we can expect in software technology, let us examine its difficulties. Following Aristotle, I divide them into *essence*—the difficulties inherent in the nature of the software—and *accidents*—those difficulties that today attend its production but that are not inherent.

The accidents I discuss in the next section. First let us consider the essence.

The essence of a software entity is a construct of interlocking concepts: data sets, relationships among data items, algorithms, and invocations of functions. This essence is abstract, in that the conceptual construct is the same under many different representations. It is nonetheless highly precise and richly detailed.

I believe the hard part of building software to be the specification, design, and testing of this conceptual construct, not the labor of representing it and testing the fidelity of the representation. We still make syntax errors, to be sure; but they are fuzz compared to the conceptual errors in most systems.

If this is true, building software will always be hard. There is inherently no silver bullet.

Let us consider the inherent properties of this irreducible essence of modern software systems: complexity, conformity, changeability, and invisibility.

Complexity.   Software entities are more complex for their size than perhaps any other human construct, because no two parts are alike (at least above the statement level). If they are, we make the two similar parts into one, a subroutine, open or closed. In this respect software systems differ profoundly from computers, buildings, or automobiles, where repeated elements abound.

Digital computers are themselves more complex than most things people build; they have very large numbers of states. This makes conceiving, describing, and testing them hard. Software systems have orders of magnitude more states than computers do.

Likewise, a scaling-up of a software entity is not merely a repetition of the same elements in larger size; it is necessarily an increase in the number of different elements. In most cases, the elements interact with each other in some nonlinear fashion, and the complexity of the whole increases much more than linearly.

The complexity of software is an essential property, not an accidental one. Hence descriptions of a software entity that abstract away its complexity often abstract away its essence. Mathematics and the physical sciences made great strides for three centuries by constructing simplified models of complex phenomena, deriving properties from the models, and verifying those properties experimentally. This worked because the complexities ignored in the models were not the essential properties of the phenomena. It does not work when the complexities are the essence.

Many of the classical problems of developing software products derive from this essential complexity and its nonlinear increases with size. From the complexity comes the difficulty of communication among team members, which leads to product flaws, cost overruns, schedule delays. From the complexity comes the difficulty of enumerating, much less understanding, all the possible states of the program, and from that comes the unreliability. From the complexity of the functions comes the difficulty of invoking those functions, which makes programs hard to use. From complexity of structure comes the difficulty of extending programs to new functions without creating side effects. From complexity of structure comes the unvisualized states that constitute security trapdoors.

Not only technical problems but management problems as well come from the complexity. This complexity makes overview hard, thus impeding conceptual integrity. It makes it hard to find and control all the loose ends. It creates the tremendous learning and understanding burden that makes personnel turnover a disaster.

Conformity.   Software people are not alone in facing complexity. Physics deals with terribly complex objects even at the "fundamental" particle level. The physicist labors on, however, in a firm faith that there are unifying principles to be found, whether in quarks or in unified field theories. Einstein repeatedly argued that there must be simplified explanations of nature, because God is not capricious or arbitrary.

No such faith comforts the software engineer. Much of the complexity he must master is arbitrary complexity, forced without rhyme or reason by the many human institutions and systems to which his interfaces must conform. These differ from interface to interface, and from time to time, not because of necessity but only because they were designed by different people, rather than by God.

In many cases the software must conform because it has most recently come to the scene. In others it must conform because it is perceived as the most conformable. But in all cases, much complexity comes from conformation to other interfaces; this cannot be simplified out by any redesign of the software alone.

Changeability.   The software entity is constantly subject to pressures for change. Of course, so are buildings, cars, computers. But manufactured things are infrequently changed after manufacture; they are superseded by later models, or essential changes are incorporated in later serial-number copies of the same basic design. Call-backs of automobiles are really quite infrequent; field changes of computers somewhat less so. Both are much less frequent than modifications to fielded software.

Partly this is because the software in a system embodies its function, and the function is the part that most feels the pressures of change. Partly it is because software can be changed more easily—it is pure thought-stuff, infinitely malleable. Buildings do in fact get changed, but the high costs of change, understood by all, serve to dampen the whims of the changers.

All successful software gets changed. Two processes are at work. As a software product is found to be useful, people try it in new cases at the edge of, or beyond, the original domain. The pressures for extended function come chiefly from users who like the basic function and invent new uses for it.

Second, successful software also survives beyond the normal life of the machine vehicle for which it is first written. If not new computers, then at least new disks, new displays, new printers come along; and the software must be conformed to its new vehicles of opportunity.

In short, the software product is embedded in a cultural matrix of applications, users, laws, and machine vehicles. These all change continually, and their changes inexorably force change upon the software product.

Invisibility. Software is invisible and unvisualizable. Geometric abstractions are powerful tools. The floor plan of a building helps both architect and client evaluate spaces, traffic flows, views. Contradictions become obvious, omissions can be caught. Scale drawings of mechanical parts and stick-figure models of molecules, although abstractions, serve the same purpose. A geometric reality is captured in a geometric abstraction.

The reality of software is not inherently embedded in space. Hence it has no ready geometric representation in the way that land has maps, silicon chips have diagrams, computers have connectivity schematics. As soon as we attempt to diagram software structure, we find it to constitute not one, but several, general directed graphs, superimposed one upon another. The several graphs may represent the flow of control, the flow of data, patterns of dependency, time sequence, name-space relationships. These are usually not even planar, much less hierarchical. Indeed, one of the ways of establishing conceptual control over such structure is to enforce link cutting until one or more of the graphs becomes hierarchical.[2]

In spite of progress in restricting and simplifying the structures of software, they remain inherently unvisualizable, thus depriving the mind of some of its most powerful conceptual tools. This lack not only impedes the process of design within one mind, it severely hinders communication among minds.

Past Breakthroughs Solved Accidental Difficulties

If we examine the three steps in software technology that have been most fruitful in the past, we discover that each attacked a different major difficulty in building software, but they have been the accidental, not the essential, difficulties. We can also see the natural limits to the extrapolation of each such attack.

High-level languages. Surely the most powerful stroke for software productivity, reliability, and simplicity has been the progressive use of high-level languages for programming. Most observers credit that development with at least a factor of five in productivity, and with concomitant gains in reliability, simplicity, and comprehensibility.

What does a high-level language accomplish? It frees a program from much of its accidental complexity. An abstract program consists of conceptual constructs: operations, datatypes, sequences, and communication. The concrete machine program is concerned with bits, registers, conditions, branches, channels, disks, and such. To the extent that the high-level language embodies the constructs wanted in the abstract program and avoids all lower ones, it eliminates a whole level of complexity that was never inherent in the program at all.

The most a high-level language can do is to furnish all the constructs the programmer imagines in the abstract program. To be sure, the level of our sophistication in thinking about data structures, data types, and operations is steadily rising, but at an ever-decreasing rate. And language development approaches closer and closer to the sophistication of users.

Moreover, at some point the elaboration of a high-level language becomes a burden that increases, not reduces, the intellectual task of the user who rarely uses the esoteric constructs.

Time-sharing. Most observers credit time-sharing with a major improvement in the productivity of programmers and in the quality of their product, although not so large as that brought by high-level languages.

Time-sharing attacks a distinctly different difficulty. Time-sharing preserves immediacy, and hence enables us to maintain an overview of complexity. The slow turnaround of batch programming means that we inevitably forget the minutiae, if not the very thrust, of what we were thinking when we stopped programming and called for compilation and execution. This interruption of consciousness is costly in time, for we must refresh. The most serious effect may well be the decay of grasp of all that is going on in a complex system.

Slow turn-around, like machine-language complexities, is an accidental rather than an essential difficulty of the software process. The limits of the contribution of time-sharing derive directly. The principal effect is to shorten system response time. As it goes to zero, at some point it passes the human threshold of noticeability, about 100 milliseconds. Beyond that no benefits are to be expected.

Unified programming environments. Unix and Interlisp, the first integrated programming environments to come into widespread use, are perceived to have improved productivity by integral factors. Why?

They attack the accidental difficulties of using programs *together*, by providing integrated libraries, unified file formats, and pipes and filters. As a result, conceptual structures that in principle could always call, feed, and use one another can indeed easily do so in practice.

This breakthrough in turn stimulated the development of whole toolbenches, since each new tool could be applied to any programs using the standard formats.

Because of these successes, environments are the subject of

much of today's software engineering research. We will look at
their promise and limitations in the next section.

Hopes for the Silver

Now let us consider the technical developments that are most
often advanced as potential silver bullets. What problems do
they address? Are they the problems of essence, or are they re-
mainders of our accidental difficulties? Do they offer revolutionary advances, or incremental ones?

Ada and other high-level language advances.   One of the most
touted recent developments is the programming language Ada,
a general-purpose, high-level language of the 1980s. Ada indeed
not only reflects evolutionary improvements in language concepts but embodies features to encourage modern design and
modularization concepts. Perhaps the Ada philosophy is more
of an advance than the Ada language, for it is the philosophy of
modularization, of abstract data types, of hierarchical structuring. Ada is perhaps over-rich, the natural product of the process
by which requirements were laid on its design. That is not fatal,
for subset working vocabularies can solve the learning problem,
and hardware advances will give us the cheap MIPS to pay for
the compiling costs. Advancing the structuring of software systems is indeed a very good use for the increased MIPS our dollars will buy. Operating systems, loudly decried in the 1960s for
their memory and cycle costs, have proved to be an excellent
form in which to use some of the MIPS and cheap memory bytes
of the past hardware surge.

Nevertheless, Ada will not prove to be the silver bullet that
slays the software productivity monster. It is, after all, just another high-level language, and the biggest payoff from such languages came from the first transition, up from the accidental
complexities of the machine into the more abstract statement
of step-by-step solutions. Once those accidents have been removed, the remaining ones are smaller, and the payoff from
their removal will surely be less.

I predict that a decade from now, when the effectiveness of Ada is assessed, it will be seen to have made a substantial difference, but not because of any particular language feature, nor indeed because of all of them combined. Neither will the new Ada environments prove to be the cause of the improvements. Ada's greatest contribution will be that switching to it occasioned training programmers in modern software design techniques.

Object-oriented programming.   Many students of the art hold out more hope for object-oriented programming than for any of the other technical fads of the day.[3] I am among them. Mark Sherman of Dartmouth notes that we must be careful to distinguish two separate ideas that go under that name: abstract data types and hierarchical types, also called *classes*. The concept of the abstract data type is that an object's type should be defined by a name, a set of proper values, and a set of proper operations, rather than its storage structure, which should be hidden. Examples are Ada packages (with private types) or Modula's modules.

Hierarchical types, such as Simula-67's classes, allow the definition of general interfaces that can be further refined by providing subordinate types. The two concepts are orthogonal—there may be hierarchies without hiding and hiding without hierarchies. Both concepts represent real advances in the art of building software.

Each removes one more accidental difficulty from the process, allowing the designer to express the essence of his design without having to express large amounts of syntactic material that add no new information content. For both abstract types and hierarchical types, the result is to remove a higher-order sort of accidental difficulty and allow a higher-order expression of design.

Nevertheless, such advances can do no more than to remove all the accidental difficulties from the expression of the design. The complexity of the design itself is essential; and such attacks make no change whatever in that. An order-of-magnitude gain can be made by object-oriented programming only if the unnecessary underbrush of type specification remaining today in our programming language is itself responsible for nine-tenths of the work involved in designing a program product. I doubt it.

Artificial intelligence.   Many people expect advances in artificial intelligence to provide the revolutionary breakthrough that will give order-of-magnitude gains in software productivity and quality.[4] I do not. To see why, we must dissect what is meant by "artificial intelligence" and then see how it applies.

Parnas has clarified the terminological chaos:

> *Two quite different definitions of AI are in common use today. AI-1: The use of computers to solve problems that previously could only be solved by applying human intelligence. AI2: The use of a specific set of programming techniques known as heuristic or rule-based programming. In this approach human experts are studied to determine what heuristics or rules of thumb they use in solving problems. . . . The program is designed to solve a problem the way that humans seem to solve it.*
>
> *The first definition has a sliding meaning. . . . Something can fit the definition of AI-1 today but, once we see how the program works and understand the problem, we will not think of it as AI anymore. . . . Unfortunately I cannot identify a body of technology that is unique to this field. . . . Most of the work is problem-specific, and some abstraction or creativity is required to see how to transfer it.*[5]

I agree completely with this critique. The techniques used for speech recognition seem to have little in common with those used for image recognition, and both are different from those used in expert systems. I have a hard time seeing how image recognition, for example, will make any appreciable difference in programming practice. The same is true of speech recognition. The hard thing about building software is deciding what to say, not saying it. No facilitation of expression can give more than marginal gains.

Expert systems technology, AI-2, deserves a section of its own.

Expert systems.   The most advanced part of the artificial intelligence art, and the most widely applied, is the technology for building expert systems. Many software scientists are hard at work applying this technology to the software-building environment.[5] What is the concept, and what are the prospects?

An expert system is a program containing a generalized inference engine and a rule base, designed to take input data and assumptions and explore the logical consequences through the inferences derivable from the rule base, yielding conclusions and advice, and offering to explain its results by retracing its reasoning for the user. The inference engines typically can deal with fuzzy or probabilistic data and rules in addition to purely deterministic logic.

Such systems offer some clear advantages over programmed algorithms for arriving at the same solutions to the same problems:

- Inference engine technology is developed in an application-independent way, and then applied to many uses. One can justify much more effort on the inference engines. Indeed, that technology is well advanced.
- The changeable parts of the application-peculiar materials are encoded in the rule base in a uniform fashion, and tools are provided for developing, changing, testing, and documenting the rule base. This regularizes much of the complexity of the application itself.

Edward Feigenbaum says that the power of such systems does not come from ever-fancier inference mechanisms, but rather from ever-richer knowledge bases that reflect the real world more accurately. I believe the most important advance offered by the technology is the separation of the application complexity from the program itself.

How can this be applied to the software task? In many ways: suggesting interface rules, advising on testing strategies, remembering bug-type frequencies, offering optimization hints, etc.

Consider an imaginary testing advisor, for example. In its most rudimentary form, the diagnostic expert system is very like a pilot's checklist, fundamentally offering suggestions as to possible causes of difficulty. As the rule base is developed, the suggestions become more specific, taking more sophisticated account of the trouble symptoms reported. One can visualize a debugging assistant that offers very generalized suggestions at first, but as more and more system structure is embodied in the rule base, becomes more and more particular in the hypotheses it generates and the tests it recommends. Such an expert system may depart most radically from the conventional ones in that its rule base should probably be hierarchically modularized in the same way the corresponding software product is, so that as the product is modularly modified, the diagnostic rule base can be modularly modified as well.

The work required to generate the diagnostic rules is work that will have to be done anyway in generating the set of test cases for the modules and for the system. If it is done in a suitably general manner, with a uniform structure for rules and a good inference engine available, it may actually reduce the total labor of generating bring-up test cases, as well as helping in lifelong maintenance and modification testing. In the same way, we can postulate other advisors—probably many of them and probably simple ones—for the other parts of the software construction task.

Many difficulties stand in the way of the early realization of useful expert advisors to the program developer. A crucial part of our imaginary scenario is the development of easy ways to get from program structure specification to the automatic or semiautomatic generation of diagnostic rules. Even more difficult and important is the twofold task of knowledge acquisition:

finding articulate, self-analytical experts who know *why* they do things; and developing efficient techniques for extracting what they know and distilling it into rule bases. The essential prerequisite for building an expert system is to have an expert.

The most powerful contribution of expert systems will surely be to put at the service of the inexperienced programmer the experience and accumulated wisdom of the best programmers. This is no small contribution. The gap between the best software engineering practice and the average practice is very wide—perhaps wider than in any other engineering discipline. A tool that disseminates good practice would be important.

"Automatic" programming.   For almost 40 years, people have been anticipating and writing about "automatic programming," the generation of a program for solving a problem from a statement of the problem specifications. Some people today write as if they expected this technology to provide the next breakthrough.[7]

Parnas implies that the term is used for glamour and not semantic content, asserting,

> In short, automatic programming always has been a euphemism for programming with a higher-level language than was presently available to the programmer.[8]

He argues, in essence, that in most cases it is the solution method, not the problem, whose specification has to be given.

Exceptions can be found. The technique of building generators is very powerful, and it is routinely used to good advantage in programs for sorting. Some systems for integrating differential equations have also permitted direct specification of the problem. The system assessed the parameters, chose from a library of methods of solution, and generated the programs.

These applications have very favorable properties:

• The problems are readily characterized by relatively few parameters.

• There are many known methods of solution to provide a library of alternatives.

- Extensive analysis has led to explicit rules for selecting solution techniques, given problem parameters.

It is hard to see how such techniques generalize to the wider
world of the ordinary software system, where cases with such
neat properties are the exception. It is hard even to imagine how
this breakthrough in generalization could conceivably occur.

Graphical programming.   A favorite subject for Ph.D. disser-
tations in software engineering is graphical, or visual, programming, the application of computer graphics to software design.[9]
Sometimes the promise of such an approach is postulated from
the analogy with VLSI chip design, where computer graphics
plays so fruitful a role. Sometimes the approach is justified by
considering flowcharts as the ideal program design medium,
and providing powerful facilities for constructing them.

Nothing even convincing, much less exciting, has yet emerged
from such efforts. I am persuaded that nothing will.

In the first place, as I have argued elsewhere, the flow chart
is a very poor abstraction of software structure.[10] Indeed, it is
best viewed as Burks, von Neumann, and Goldstine's attempt
to provide a desperately needed high-level control language for
their proposed computer. In the pitiful, multipage, connection-
boxed form to which the flow chart has today been elaborated,
it has proved to be essentially useless as a design tool—programmers draw flow charts after, not before, writing the programs they describe.

Second, the screens of today are too small, in pixels, to
show both the scope and the resolution of any serious detailed
software diagram. The so-called "desktop metaphor" of today's
workstation is instead an "airplane-seat" metaphor. Anyone
who has shuffled a lapful of papers while seated in coach
between two portly passengers will recognize the difference—
one can see only a very few things at once. The true desktop
provides overview of and random access to a score of pages.
Moreover, when fits of creativity run strong, more than one programmer or writer has been known to abandon the desktop for

the more spacious floor. The hardware technology will have to advance quite substantially before the scope of our scopes is sufficient to the software design task.

More fundamentally, as I have argued above, software is very difficult to visualize. Whether we diagram control flow, variable scope nesting, variable cross-references, data flow, hierarchical data structures, or whatever, we feel only one dimension of the intricately interlocked software elephant. If we superimpose all the diagrams generated by the many relevant views, it is difficult to extract any global overview. The VLSI analogy is fundamentally misleading—a chip design is a layered two-dimensional object whose geometry reflects its essence. A software system is not.

Program verification.   Much of the effort in modern programming goes into the testing and repair of bugs. Is there perhaps a silver bullet to be found by eliminating the errors at the source, in the system design phase? Can both productivity and product reliability be radically enhanced by following the profoundly different strategy of proving designs correct before the immense effort is poured into implementing and testing them?

I do not believe we will find the magic here. Program verification is a very powerful concept, and it will be very important for such things as secure operating system kernels. The technology does not promise, however, to save labor. Verifications are so much work that only a few substantial programs have ever been verified.

Program verification does not mean error-proof programs. There is no magic here, either. Mathematical proofs also can be faulty. So whereas verification might reduce the program-testing load, it cannot eliminate it.

More seriously, even perfect program verification can only establish that a program meets its specification. The hardest part of the software task is arriving at a complete and consistent specification, and much of the essence of building a program is in fact the debugging of the specification.

Environments and tools. How much more gain can be expected from the exploding researches into better programming environments? One's instinctive reaction is that the big-payoff problems were the first attacked, and have been solved: hierarchical file systems, uniform file formats so as to have uniform program interfaces, and generalized tools. Language-specific smart editors are developments not yet widely used in practice, but the most they promise is freedom from syntactic errors and simple semantic errors.

Perhaps the biggest gain yet to be realized in the programming environment is the use of integrated database systems to keep track of the myriads of details that must be recalled accurately by the individual programmer and kept current in a group of collaborators on a single system.

Surely this work is worthwhile, and surely it will bear some fruit in both productivity and reliability. But by its very nature, the return from now on must be marginal.

Workstations.   What gains are to be expected for the software art from the certain and rapid increase in the power and memory capacity of the individual workstation? Well, how many MIPS can one use fruitfully? The composition and editing of programs and documents is fully supported by today's speeds. Compiling could stand a boost, but a factor of 10 in machine speed would surely leave think-time the dominant activity in the programmer's day. Indeed, it appears to be so now.

More powerful workstations we surely welcome. Magical enhancements from them we cannot expect.

Promising Attacks on the Conceptual Essence

Even though no technological breakthrough promises to give the sort of magical results with which we are so familiar in the hardware area, there is both an abundance of good work going on now, and the promise of steady, if unspectacular progress.

All of the technological attacks on the accidents of the software process are fundamentally limited by the productivity equation:

$$Time\ of\ task\ =\ \sum_i (Frequency)_i \times (Time)_i$$

If, as I believe, the conceptual components of the task are now taking most of the time, then no amount of activity on the task components that are merely the expression of the concepts can give large productivity gains.

Hence we must consider those attacks that address the essence of the software problem, the formulation of these complex conceptual structures. Fortunately, some of these are very promising.

Buy versus build.   The most radical possible solution for constructing software is not to construct it at all.

Every day this becomes easier, as more and more vendors offer more and better software products for a dizzying variety of applications. While we software engineers have labored on production methodology, the personal computer revolution has created not one, but many, mass markets for software. Every newsstand carries monthly magazines which, sorted by machine type, advertise and review dozens of products at prices from a few dollars to a few hundred dollars. More specialized sources offer very powerful products for the workstation and other Unix markets. Even software tools and environments can be bought off-the-shelf. I have elsewhere proposed a marketplace for individual modules.

Any such product is cheaper to buy than to build afresh. Even at a cost of $100,000, a purchased piece of software is costing only about as much as one programmer-year. And delivery is immediate! Immediate at least for products that really exist, products whose developer can refer the prospect to a happy user. Moreover, such products tend to be much better documented and somewhat better maintained than homegrown software.

The development of the mass market is, I believe, the most profound long-run trend in software engineering. The cost of software has always been development cost, not replication cost. Sharing that cost among even a few users radically cuts the per-user cost. Another way of looking at it is that the use of n copies of a software system effectively multiplies the productivity of its developers by n. That is an enhancement of the productivity of the discipline and of the nation.

The key issue, of course, is applicability. Can I use an available off-the-shelf package to do my task? A surprising thing has happened here. During the 1950s and 1960s, study after study showed that users would not use off-the-shelf packages for payroll, inventory control, accounts receivable, etc. The requirements were too specialized, the case-to-case variation too high. During the 1980s, we find such packages in high demand and widespread use. What has changed?

Not really the packages. They may be somewhat more generalized and somewhat more customizable than formerly, but not much. Not really the applications, either. If anything, the business and scientific needs of today are more diverse, more complicated than those of 20 years ago.

The big change has been in the hardware/software cost ratio. The buyer of a $2-million machine in 1960 felt that he could afford $250,000 more for a customized payroll program, one that slipped easily and nondisruptively into the computer-hostile social environment. Buyers of $50,000 office machines today cannot conceivably afford customized payroll programs; so they adapt their payroll procedures to the packages available. Computers are now so commonplace, if not yet so beloved, that the adaptations are accepted as a matter of course.

There are dramatic exceptions to my argument that the generalization of the software packages has changed little over the years: electronic spreadsheets and simple database systems. These powerful tools, so obvious in retrospect and yet so late appearing, lend themselves to myriad uses, some quite unorthodox. Articles and even books now abound on how to tackle unexpected tasks with the spreadsheet. Large numbers of applications that would formerly have been written as custom programs in Cobol or Report Program Generator are now routinely done with these tools.

Many users now operate their own computers day in and day out on varied applications without ever writing a program. Indeed, many of these users cannot write new programs for their machines, but they are nevertheless adept at solving new problems with them.

I believe the single most powerful software productivity strategy for many organizations today is to equip the computer-naive intellectual workers on the firing line with personal computers and good generalized writing, drawing, file, and spreadsheet programs, and turn them loose. The same strategy, with generalized mathematical and statistical packages and some simple programming capabilities, will also work for hundreds of laboratory scientists.

Requirements refinement and rapid prototyping.   The hardest single part of building a software system is deciding precisely what to build. No other part of the conceptual work is so difficult as establishing the detailed technical requirements, including all the interfaces to people, to machines, and to other software systems. No other part of the work so cripples the resulting system if done wrong. No other part is more difficult to rectify later.

Therefore the most important function that software builders do for their clients is the iterative extraction and refinement of the product requirements. For the truth is, the clients do not know what they want. They usually do not know what questions must be answered, and they almost never have thought of the problem in the detail that must be specified. Even the simple answer—"Make the new software system work like our old manual information-processing system"—is in fact too simple. Clients never want exactly that. Complex software systems are, moreover, things that act, that move, that work. The dynamics of that action are hard to imagine. So in planning any software activity, it is necessary to allow for an extensive iteration between the client and the designer as part of the system definition.

I would go a step further and assert that it is really impossible for clients, even those working with software engineers, to specify completely, precisely, and correctly the exact requirements of a modern software product before having built and tried some versions of the product they are specifying.

Therefore one of the most promising of the current technological efforts, and one which attacks the essence, not the accidents, of the software problem, is the development of approaches and tools for rapid prototyping of systems as part of the iterative specification of requirements.

A prototype software system is one that simulates the important interfaces and performs the main functions of the intended system, while not being necessarily bound by the same hardware speed, size, or cost constraints. Prototypes typically perform the mainline tasks of the application, but make no attempt to handle the exceptions, respond correctly to invalid inputs, abort cleanly, etc. The purpose of the prototype is to make real the conceptual structure specified, so that the client can test it for consistency and usability.

Much of present-day software acquisition procedures rests upon the assumption that one can specify a satisfactory system in advance, get bids for its construction, have it built, and install it. I think this assumption is fundamentally wrong, and that many software acquisition problems spring from that fallacy. Hence they cannot be fixed without fundamental revision, one that provides for iterative development and specification of prototypes and products.

Incremental development—grow, not build, software.   I still remember the jolt I felt in 1958 when I first heard a friend talk about *building* a program, as opposed to *writing* one. In a flash he broadened my whole view of the software process. The metaphor shift was powerful, and accurate. Today we understand how like other building processes the construction of software is, and we freely use other elements of the metaphor, such as *specifications, assembly of components,* and *scaffolding.*

The building metaphor has outlived its usefulness. It is time to change again. If, as I believe, the conceptual structures we construct today are too complicated to be accurately specified in advance, and too complex to be built faultlessly, then we must take a radically different approach.

Let us turn to nature and study complexity in living things, instead of just the dead works of man. Here we find constructs whose complexities thrill us with awe. The brain alone is intricate beyond mapping, powerful beyond imitation, rich in diversity, self-protecting, and self-renewing. The secret is that it is grown, not built.

So it must be with our software systems. Some years ago Harlan Mills proposed that any software system should be grown by incremental development.[11] That is, the system should first be made to run, even though it does nothing useful except call the proper set of dummy subprograms. Then, bit by bit it is fleshed out, with the subprograms in turn being developed into actions or calls to empty stubs in the level below.

I have seen the most dramatic results since I began urging this technique on the project builders in my software engineering laboratory class. Nothing in the past decade has so radically changed my own practice, or its effectiveness. The approach necessitates top-down design, for it is a top-down growing of the software. It allows easy backtracking. It lends itself to early prototypes. Each added function and new provision for more complex data or circumstances grows organically out of what is already there.

The morale effects are startling. Enthusiasm jumps when there is a running system, even a simple one. Efforts redouble when the first picture from a new graphics software system appears on the screen, even if it is only a rectangle. One always has, at every stage in the process, a working system. I find that teams can *grow* much more complex entities in four months than they can *build*.

The same benefits can be realized on large projects as on my small ones.[12]

Great designers.   The central question of how to improve the software art centers, as it always has, on people.

We can get good designs by following good practices instead of poor ones. Good design practices can be taught. Programmers are among the most intelligent part of the population, so they can learn good practice. Thus a major thrust in the United States is to promulgate good modern practice. New curricula, new literature, new organizations such as the Software Engineering Institute, all have come into being in order to raise the level of our practice from poor to good. This is entirely proper.

Nevertheless, I do not believe we can make the next step upward in the same way. Whereas the difference between poor conceptual designs and good ones may lie in the soundness of design method, the difference between good designs and great ones surely does not. Great designs come from great designers. Software construction is a *creative* process. Sound methodology can empower and liberate the creative mind; it cannot enflame or inspire the drudge.

The differences are not minor—it is rather like Salieri and Mozart. Study after study shows that the very best designers produce structures that are faster, smaller, simpler, cleaner, and produced with less effort. The differences between the great and the average approach an order of magnitude.

A little retrospection shows that although many fine, useful software systems have been designed by committees and built by multipart projects, those software systems that have excited passionate fans are those that are the products of one or a few designing minds, great designers. Consider Unix, APL, Pascal, Modula, the Smalltalk interface, even Fortran; and contrast with Cobol, PL/I, Algol, MVS/370, and MS-DOS (Fig. 16.1).

Hence, although I strongly support the technology transfer and curriculum development efforts now underway, I think the most important single effort we can mount is to develop ways to grow great designers.

No software organization can ignore this challenge. Good managers, scarce though they be, are no scarcer than good de-

Yes	No
Unix	Cobol
APL	PL/1
Pascal	Algol
Modula	MVS/370
Smalltalk	MS-DOS
Fortran	

Fig. 16.1   Exciting products

signers. Great designers and great managers are both very rare. Most organizations spend considerable effort in finding and cultivating the management prospects; I know of none that spends equal effort in finding and developing the great designers upon whom the technical excellence of the products will ultimately depend.

My first proposal is that each software organization must determine and proclaim that great designers are as important to its success as great managers are, and that they can be expected to be similarly nurtured and rewarded. Not only salary, but the perquisites of recognition—office size, furnishings, personal technical equipment, travel funds, staff support—must be fully equivalent.

How to grow great designers? Space does not permit a lengthy discussion, but some steps are obvious:

- Systematically identify top designers as early as possible. The best are often not the most experienced.
- Assign a career mentor to be responsible for the development of the prospect, and keep a careful career file.
- Devise and maintain a career development plan for each prospect, including carefully selected apprenticeships with top designers, episodes of advanced formal education, and short courses, all interspersed with solo design and technical leadership assignments.
- Provide opportunities for growing designers to interact with and stimulate each other.

17
"No Silver Bullet" Refired

17
"No Silver Bullet" Refired

Every bullet has its billet.

WILLIAM III OF ENGLAND, PRINCE OF ORANGE

Whoever thinks a faultless piece to see,
Thinks what ne'er was, nor is, nor e'er shall be.

ALEXANDER POPE, AN ESSAY ON CRITICISM

Assembling a structure from ready-made parts, 1945
The Bettman Archive

On Werewolves and Other Legendary Terrors

"No Silver Bullet—Essence and Accidents of Software Engineering" (now Chapter 16) was originally an invited paper for the IFIP '86 conference in Dublin, and it was published in those proceedings.[1] *Computer* magazine reprinted it, behind a gothic cover, illustrated with stills from films such as *The Werewolf of London*.[2] They also provided an explanatory sidebar "To Slay the Werewolf," setting forth the (modern) legend that only silver bullets will do. I was not aware of the sidebar and illustrations before publication, and I never expected a serious technical paper to be so embellished.

Computer's editors were expert in achieving their desired effect, however, and many people seem to have read the paper. I have therefore chosen yet another werewolf picture for that chapter, an ancient depiction of an almost comical creature. I hope this less garish picture will have the same salutary effect.

There is Too a Silver Bullet—AND HERE IT IS!

"No Silver Bullet" asserts and argues that no single software engineering development will produce an order-of-magnitude improvement in programming productivity within ten years (from the paper's publication in 1986). We are now nine years into that decade, so it is timely to see how this prediction is holding up.

Whereas *The Mythical Man-Month* generated many citations but little argument, "No Silver Bullet" has occasioned rebuttal papers, letters to journal editors, and letters and essays that continue to this day.[3] Most of these attack the central argument that there is no magical solution, and my clear opinion that there cannot be one. Most agree with most of the arguments in "NSB," but then go on to assert that there is indeed a silver bullet for the software beast, which the author has invented. As I reread the early responses today, I can't help noticing that the nostrums pushed so vigorously in 1986 and 1987 have not had the dramatic effects claimed.

I buy hardware and software chiefly by the "happy user" test—conversations with *bona fide* cash-paying customers who use the product and are pleased. Likewise, I shall most readily believe a silver bullet has materialized when a *bona fide* independent user steps forth and says, "I used this methodology, tool, or product, and it gave me a tenfold improvement in software productivity."

Many correspondents have made valid emendations or clarifications. Some have undertaken point-by-point analysis and rebuttal, for which I am grateful. In this chapter, I shall share the improvements and address the rebuttals.

Obscure Writing Will Be Misunderstood

Some writers show that I failed to make some arguments clear.

Accident.   The central argument of "NSB" is as clearly stated in the Abstract to Chapter 16 as I know how to put it. Some have been confused, however, by the terms *accident* and *accidental*, which follow an ancient usage going back to Aristotle.[4] By *accidental*, I did not mean *occurring by chance*, nor *misfortunate*, but more nearly *incidental*, or *appurtenant*.

I would not denigrate the accidental parts of software construction; instead I follow the English dramatist, detective story writer, and theologian Dorothy Sayers in seeing all creative activity to consist of (1) the formulation of the conceptual constructs, (2) implementation in real media, and (3) interactivity with users in real uses.[5] The part of software building I called *essence* is the mental crafting of the conceptual construct; the part I called *accident* is its implementation process.

A question of fact.   It seems to me (although not to everyone) that the truthfulness of the central argument boils down to a question of fact: What fraction of total software effort is now associated with the accurate and orderly representation of the conceptual construct, and what fraction is the effort of mentally crafting the constructs? The finding and fixing of flaws falls partly in each fraction, according to whether the flaws are conceptual, such as failing to recognize some exception, or representational, such as a pointer mistake or a memory allocation mistake.

It is my opinion, and that is all, that the accidental or representational part of the work is now down to about half or less of the total. Since this fraction is a question of fact, its value could in principle be settled by measurement.[6] Failing that, my estimate of it can be corrected by better informed and more current estimates. Significantly, no one who has written publicly or privately has asserted that the accidental part is as large as 9/10.

"NSB" argues, indisputably, that if the accidental part of the work is less than 9/10 of the total, shrinking it to zero (which *would* take magic) will not give an order of magnitude productivity improvement. One *must* attack the essence.

Since "NSB," Bruce Blum has drawn my attention to the 1959 work of Herzberg, Mausner, and Sayderman.[7] They find that motivational factors *can* increase productivity. On the other hand, environmental and accidental factors, no matter how positive, cannot; but these factors can decrease productivity when negative. "NSB" argues that much software progress has been the removal of such negative factors: stunningly awkward machine languages, batch processing with long turnaround times, poor tools, and severe memory constraints.

Are the *essential* difficulties therefore *hopeless*? An excellent 1990 paper by Brad Cox, "There Is a Silver Bullet," argues eloquently for the reusable, interchangeable component approach as an attack on the conceptual essence of the problem.[8] I enthusiastically agree.

Cox however misunderstands "NSB" on two points. First, he reads it as asserting that software difficulties arise "from some deficiency in how programmers build software today." My argument was that the essential difficulties are inherent in the conceptual complexity of the software functions to be designed and built at any time, by any method. Second, he (and others) read "NSB" as asserting that there is no hope of attacking the essential difficulties of software building. That was not my intent. Crafting the conceptual construct does indeed have as inherent difficulties complexity, conformity, changeability, and invisibility. The troubles caused by each of these difficulties can, however, be ameliorated.

Complexity is by levels.   For example, complexity is the most serious inherent difficulty, but not all complexity is inevitable. Much, but not all, of the conceptual complexity in our software constructs comes from the arbitrary complexity of the applications themselves. Indeed, Lars Sødahl of MYSIGMA Sødahl and Partners, a multinational management consulting firm, writes:

> In my experience most of the complexities which are encountered in systems work are symptoms of organizational malfunctions. Trying to model this reality with equally complex programs is actually to conserve the mess instead of solving the problems.

Steve Lukasik of Northrop argues that even organizational complexity is perhaps not arbitrary but may be susceptible to ordering principles:

> I trained as a physicist and thus see "complex" things as susceptible to description in terms of simpler concepts. Now you may be right; I will not assert that all complex things are susceptible to ordering principles. . . . by the same rules of argument you cannot assert that they can not be.

> . . .Yesterday's complexity is tomorrow's order. The complexity of molecular disorder gave way to the kinetic theory of gases and the three laws of thermodynamics. Now software may not ever reveal those kinds of ordering principles, but the burden is on you to explain why not. I am not being obtuse or argumentative. I believe that someday the "complexity" of software will be understood in terms of some higher order notions (invariants to the physicist).

I have not undertaken the deeper analysis Lukasik properly calls for. As a discipline, we need an extended information theory that quantifies the information content of static structures, just as Shannon's theory does for communicated streams. That is quite beyond me. To Lukasik I simply respond that system complexity is a function of myriad details that must each be specified exactly, either by some general rule or detail-by-detail, but not just statistically. It seems very unlikely that uncoordinated works of many minds should have enough coherence to be exactly described by general rules.

Much of the complexity in a software construct is, however, not due to conformity to the external world but rather to the implementation itself—its data structures, its algorithms, its connectivity. Growing software in higher-level chunks, built by someone else or reused from one's own past, avoids facing whole layers of complexity. "NSB" advocates a wholehearted attack on the problem of complexity, quite optimistic that progress can be made. It advocates adding necessary complexity to a software system:

- Hierarchically, by layered modules or objects
- Incrementally, so that the system always works.

Harel's Analysis

David Harel, in the 1992 paper, "Biting the Silver Bullet," undertakes the most careful analysis of "NSB" that has been published.[9]

Pessimism vs. optimism vs. realism.   Harel sees both "NSB" and Parnas's 1984 "Software Aspects of Strategic Defense Systems,"[10] as "far too bleak." So he aims to illuminate the brighter side of the coin, subtitling his paper "Toward a Brighter Future for System Development." Cox as well as Harel reads "NSB" as pessimistic, and he says, "But if you view these same facts from a new perspective, a more optimistic conclusion emerges." Both misread the tone.

First, my wife, my colleagues, and my editors find me to err far more often in optimism than in pessimism. I am, after all, a programmer by background, and optimism is an occupational disease of our craft.

"NSB" says explicitly "As we look to the horizon of a decade hence, we see no silver bullet. . . . Skepticism is not pessimism, however. . . . There is no royal road, but there is a road." It forecasts that the innovations under way in 1986, if developed and exploited, would *together* indeed achieve an order-of-magnitude improvement in productivity. As the 1986–1996 decade proceeds, this prediction appears, if anything, too optimistic rather than too gloomy.

Even if "NSB" were universally seen as pessimistic, what is wrong with that? Is Einstein's statement that nothing can travel faster than the speed of light "bleak" or "gloomy?" How about Gödel's result that some things cannot be computed? "NSB" undertakes to establish that "the very nature of software makes it unlikely that there will ever be any silver bullets." Turski, in his excellent response paper at the IFIP Conference, said eloquently:

> *Of all misguided scientific endeavours, none are more pathetic than the search for the philosophers' stone, a substance supposed to change base metals into gold. The supreme object of alchemy, ardently pursued by generations of researchers generously funded by secular and spiritual rulers, is an undiluted extract of wishful thinking, of the common assumption that things are as we would like them to be. It is a very human belief. It takes a lot of effort to accept the existence of insoluble problems. The wish to see a way out, against all odds, even when it is proven that it does not exist, is very, very strong. And most of us have a lot of sympathy for these courageous souls who try to achieve the impossible. And so it continues. Dissertations on squaring a circle are being written. Lotions to restore lost hair are concocted and sell well. Methods to improve software productivity are hatched and sell very well.*

All too often we are inclined to follow our own optimism (or exploit the optimistic hopes of our sponsors). All too often we are willing to disregard the voice of reason and heed the siren calls of panacea pushers. [11]

Turski and I both insist that pipe-dreaming *inhibits forward progress and wastes effort.*

"Gloom" themes.   Harel perceives gloom in "NSB" to arise from three themes:

- Sharp separation into essence and accident
- Treatment of each silver bullet candidate in isolation
- Predicting for only 10 years, instead of a long enough time in which "to expect any significant improvement."

As to the first, that is the whole point of the paper. I still believe this separation is absolutely central to understanding why software is hard. It is a sure guide as to what kinds of attacks to make.

As to treating candidate bullets in isolation, "NSB" does so indeed. The various candidates have been proposed one by one, with extravagant claims for each one *by itself.* It is fair to assess them one by one. It is not the techniques I oppose, it is expecting them to work magic. Glass, Vessey, and Conger in their 1992 paper offer ample evidence that the vain search for a silver bullet has not yet ended. [12]

As to choosing 10 years versus 40 years as a prediction period, the shorter period was in part a concession that our predictive powers have never been good beyond a decade. Which of us in 1975 predicted the microcomputer revolution of the 1980s?

There are other reasons for the decade limit: the claims made for candidate bullets all have had a certain immediacy about them. I recollect none that said "Invest in my nostrum, and you will start winning after 10 years." Moreover, hardware performance/price ratios have improved by perhaps a hundredfold per decade, and the comparison, though quite invalid, is subconsciously inevitable. We will surely make substantial progress over the next 40 years; an order of magnitude over 40 years is hardly magical.

Harel's thought experiment.   Harel proposes a thought experiment in which he postulates "NSB" as having been written in 1952, instead of 1986, but asserting the same propositions. This he uses as a *reducto ad absurdum* to argue against attempting to separate essence from accident.

The argument doesn't work. First, "NSB" begins by asserting that the accidental difficulties grossly dominated the essential ones in 1950s programming, that they no longer do so, and that eliminating them has effected orders-of-magnitude improvements. Translating that argument back 40 years is unreasonable; one can hardly imagine asserting in 1952 that the accidental difficulties do not occasion a major part of the effort.

Second, the state of affairs Harel imagines to have prevailed in the 1950s is inaccurate:

> *That was the time when instead of grappling with the design of large, complex systems, programmers were in the business of developing conventional one-person programs (which would be on the order of 100–200 lines in a modern programming language) that were to carry out limited algorithmic tasks. Given the technology and methodology available then, such tasks were similarly formidable. Failures, errors, and missed deadlines were all around.*

He then describes how the postulated failures, errors, and missed deadlines in the conventional little one-person programs were improved by an order of magnitude over the next 25 years.

But the state of the art in the 1950s was not in fact small one-person programs. In 1952, the Univac was at work processing the 1950 census with a complex program developed by about eight programmers.[13] Other machines were doing chemical dynamics, neutron diffusion calculations, missile performance calculations, etc.[14] Assemblers, relocating linkers and loaders, floating-point interpretive systems, etc. were in routine use.[15]

By 1955 people were building 50 to 100 man-year business programs.[16] By 1956 General Electric had in operation a payroll system in its Louisville appliance plant with more than 80,000 words of program. By 1957, the SAGE ANFSQ/7 air defense computer had been running two years, and a 75,000 instruction communications-based, fail-safe-duplexed real-time system was in operation in 30 sites.[17] One can hardly maintain that it is evolution of techniques for one-person programs that chiefly describes software engineering efforts since 1952.

AND HERE IT IS.   Harel goes on to offer his own silver bullet, a modeling technique called "The Vanilla Framework." The approach itself is not described in enough detail for evaluation, but reference is given to a paper, and to a technical report to appear in book form in due time.[18] Modeling does address the essence, the proper crafting and debugging of concepts, so it is possible that the Vanilla Framework will be revolutionary. I hope so. Ken Brooks reports he found it a helpful methodology when he tried it for a real task.

Invisibility.   Harel argues strongly that much of the conceptual construct of software is inherently topological in nature and these relationships have natural counterparts in spatial/graphical representations:

> *Using appropriate visual formalisms can have a spectacular effect on engineers and programmers. Moreover, this effect is not limited to mere accidental issues; the quality and expedition of their very thinking was found to be improved. Successful system development in the future will revolve around visual representations. We will first conceptualize, using the "proper" entities and relationships, and then formulate and reformulate our conceptions as a series of increasingly more comprehensive models represented in an appropriate combination of visual languages. A combination it must be, since system models have several facets, each of which conjures up different kinds of mental images.*

. . . . Some aspects of the modeling process have not been as forth-coming as others in lending themselves to good visualization. Algorithmic operations on variables and data structures, for example, will probably remain textual.

Harel and I are quite close. What I argued is that software structure is not embedded in three-space, so there is no natural single mapping from a conceptual design to a diagram, whether in two dimensions or more. He concedes, and I agree, that one needs multiple diagrams, each covering some distinct aspect, and that some aspects don't diagram well at all.

I completely share his enthusiasm for using diagrams as thought and design aids. I have long enjoyed asking candidate programmers, "Where is next November?" If the question is too cryptic, then, "Tell me about your mental model of the calendar." The really good programmers have strong spatial senses; they usually have geometric models of time; and they quite often understand the first question without elaboration. They have highly individualistic models.

Jones's Point—Productivity *Follows* Quality

Capers Jones, writing first in a series of memoranda and later in a book, offers a penetrating insight, which has been stated by several of my correspondents. "NSB," like most writings at the time, was focused on *productivity,* the software output per unit of input. Jones says, "No. Focus on *quality,* and productivity will follow."[19] He argues that costly and late projects invest most of the extra work and time in finding and repairing errors in specification, in design, in implementation. He offers data that show a strong correlation between lack of systematic quality controls and schedule disasters. I believe it. Boehm points out that productivity drops again as one pursues extreme quality, as in IBM's space-shuttle software.

Coqui similarly argues that systematic software development disciplines were developed in response to quality concerns (especially avoidance of major disasters) rather than productivity concerns.

> *But note: the goal of applying Engineering principles to Software production in the 1970s was to increase the Quality, Testability, Stability, and Predictability of software products—not necessarily the efficiency of Software production.*

> *The driving force to use Software Engineering principles in software production was the fear of major accidents that might be caused by having uncontrollable artists responsible for the development of ever more complex systems.*[20]

So What Has Happened to Productivity?

Productivity numbers.   Productivity numbers are very hard to define, hard to calibrate, and hard to find. Capers Jones believes that for two equivalent COBOL programs written 10 years apart, one without structured methodology and one with, the gain is a factor of three.

Ed Yourdon says, "I see people getting a fivefold improvement due to workstations and software tools." Tom DeMarco believes "Your expectation of an order-of-magnitude improvement in 10 years, due to the whole basket of techniques, was optimistic. I haven't seen organizations making an order-of-magnitude improvement."

Shrink-wrapped software—Buy; don't build.   One 1986 assessment in "NSB" has, I think, proved to be correct: "The development of the mass market is . . . the most profound long-run trend in software engineering." From the discipline's viewpoint, the mass-market software is almost a new industry compared to that of the development of custom software, whether in-house or out-house. When packages sell in the millions—or even the thousands—quality, timeliness, product performance, and support cost become dominant issues, rather than the development cost that is so crucial for custom systems.

Power tools for the mind.   The most dramatic way to improve
the productivity of management information systems (MIS) programmers is to go down to your local computer store and buy
off the shelf what they would have built. This is not ridiculous;
the availability of cheap, powerful shrink-wrapped software has
met many needs that formerly would have occasioned custom
packages. These power tools for the mind are more like electric
drills, saws, and sanders than they are like big complex production tools. The integration of these into compatible and cross-
linked sets such as Microsoft Works and the better-integrated
ClarisWorks give immense flexibility. And like the homeowner's
collection of power hand tools, frequent use of a small set, for
many different tasks, develops familiarity. Such tools must emphasize ease of use for the casual user, not the professional.

Ivan Selin, Chairman of American Management Systems,
Inc., wrote me in 1987:

> *I quibble with your statement that packages have not really changed
> that much. . . . I think you too lightly throw off the major impli-
> cations of your observation that, [the software packages] "may be
> somewhat more generalized and somewhat more customizable than
> formerly, but not much." Even accepting this statement at face
> value, I believe that the users see the packages as being both more
> generalized and easier to customize, and that this perception leads
> the users to be much more amenable to packages. In most cases that
> my company finds, it is the [end] users, not the software people,
> who are reluctant to use packages because they think they will lose
> essential features or functions, and hence the prospect of easy cus-
> tomization is a big selling point to them.*

I think Selin is quite right—I underestimated both the degree of
package customizability and its importance.

Object-Oriented Programming—Will a Brass Bullet Do?

Building with bigger pieces.   The illustration opening this
chapter reminds us that if one assembles a set of pieces, each of

which may be complex, and all of which are designed to have smooth interfaces, quite rich structures go together rapidly.

One view of object-oriented programming is that it is a discipline that enforces *modularity* and clean interfaces. A second view emphasizes *encapsulation*, the fact that one cannot see, much less design, the inner structure of the pieces. Another view emphasizes *inheritance*, with its concomitant *hierarchical* structure of classes, with virtual functions. Yet another view emphasizes *strong abstract data-typing*, with its assurance that a particular data-type will be manipulated only by operations proper to it.

Now any of these disciplines can be had without taking the whole Smalltalk or C++ package—many of them predated object-oriented technology. The attractiveness of object-oriented approach is that of a multivitamin pill: in one fell swoop (that is, programmer retraining), one gets them all. It is a very promising concept.

Why has object-oriented technique grown slowly?   In the nine years since "NSB," the expectancy has steadily grown. Why has growth been slow? Theories abound. James Coggins, author for four years of the column, "The Best of comp.lang.c++" in *The C++ Report*, offers this explanation:

> *The problem is that programmers in O-O have been experimenting in incestuous applications and aiming low in abstraction, instead of high. For example, they have been building classes such as* linked-list *or* set *instead of classes such as* user-interface *or* radiation beam *or* finite-element model. *Unfortunately the selfsame strong type-checking in C++ that helps programmers to avoid errors also makes it hard to build big things out of little ones.*[21]

He goes back to the basic software problem, and argues that one way to address unmet software needs is to increase the size of the intelligent workforce by enabling and coopting our clients. This argues for top-down design:

If we design large-grained classes that address concepts our clients are already working with, they can understand and question the design as it grows, and they can cooperate in the design of test cases. My ophthalmology collaborators don't care about stacks; they do care about Legendre polynomial shape descriptions of corneas. Small encapsulations yield small benefits.

David Parnas, whose paper was one of the origins of object-oriented concepts, sees the matter differently. He writes me:

The answer is simple. It is because [O-O] has been tied to a variety of complex languages. Instead of teaching people that O-O is a type of design, and giving them design principles, people have taught that O-O is the use of a particular tool. We can write good or bad programs with any tool. Unless we teach people how to design, the languages matter very little. The result is that people do bad designs with these languages and get very little value from them. If the value is small, it won't catch on.

Front-loaded costs, down-stream benefits.   My own belief is that object-oriented techniques have a peculiarly severe case of a malady that characterizes many methodological improvements. The up-front costs are very substantial—primarily retraining programmers to think in a quite new way, but also extra investment in fashioning functions into generalized classes. The benefits, which I think are real and not merely putative, occur all along the development cycle; but the big benefits pay off during successor building, extension, and maintenance activities. Coggins says, "Object-oriented techniques will not make the first project development any faster, or the next one. The fifth one in that family will go blazingly fast."[22]

Betting real up-front money for the sake of projected but iffy benefits later is what investors do every day. In many programming organizations, however, it requires real managerial courage, a commodity much scarcer than technical competence or administrative proficiency. I believe the extreme degree of cost front-loading and benefit back-loading is the largest single factor slowing the adoption of O-O techniques. Even so, C++ seems to be steadily replacing C in many communities.

What About Reuse?

The best way to attack the essence of building software is not to build it at all. Package software is only one of the ways of doing this. Program reuse is another. Indeed, the promise of easy reuse of classes, with easy customization via inheritance, is one of the strongest attractions of object-oriented techniques.

As is so often the case, as one gets some experience with a new way of doing business the new mode is not so simple as first appears.

Of course, programmers have always reused their own handiwork. Jones says,

> Most experienced programmers have private libraries which allow them to develop software with about 30% reused code by volume. Reusability at the corporate level aims for 75% reused code by volume, and requires special library and administrative support. Corporate reusable code also implies changes in project accounting and measurement practices to give credit for reusability.[23]

W. Huang proposed organizing software factories with a matrix management of functional specialists, so as to harness the natural propensity of each to reuse his own code.[24]

Van Snyder of JPL points out to me that the mathematical software community has a long tradition of reusing software:

> We conjecture that barriers to reuse are not on the producer side, but on the consumer side. If a software engineer, a potential consumer of standardized software components, perceives it to be more expensive to find a component that meets his need, and so verify, than to write one anew, a new, duplicative component will be written. Notice we said perceives above. It doesn't matter what the true cost of reconstruction is.

Reuse has been successful for mathematical software for two rea-sons: (1) It is arcane, requiring an enormous intellectual input per line of code; and (2) there is a rich and standard nomenclature, namely mathematics, to describe the functionality of each compo-nent. Thus the cost to reconstruct a component of mathematical software is high, and the cost to discover the functionality of an existing component is low. The long tradition of professional jour-nals publishing and collecting algorithms, and offering them at modest cost, and commercial concerns offering very high quality algorithms at somewhat higher but still modest cost, makes discov-ering a component that meets one's need simpler than in many other disciplines, where it is sometimes not possible to specify one's need precisely and tersely. These factors collaborate to make it more attractive to reuse rather than to reinvent mathematical software.

The same reuse phenomenon is found among several com-munities, such as those that build codes for nuclear reactors, cli-mate models, and ocean models, and for the same reasons. The communities each grew up with the same textbooks and stan-dard notations.

How does corporate-level reuse fare today?   Lots of study; rel-atively little practice in the United States; anecdotal reports of more reuse abroad.[25]

Jones reports that all of his firm's clients with over 5000 pro-grammers have formal reuse research, whereas fewer than 10 percent of the clients with under 500 programmers do.[26] He re-ports that in industries with the greatest reuse potential, reus-ability research (not deployment) "is active and energetic, even if not yet totally successful." Ed Yourdon reports a software house in Manila that has 50 of its 200 programmers building only reusable modules for the rest to use; "I've seen a few cases—adoption is due to *organizational* factors such as the re-ward structure, not technical factors."

DeMarco tells me that the availability of mass-market pack-ages and their suitability as providers of generic functions such as database systems has substantially reduced both the pressure and the marginal utility of reusing modules of one's application code. "The reusable modules tended to be the generic functions anyway."

Parnas writes,

> *Reuse is something that is far easier to say than to do. Doing it requires both good design and very good documentation. Even when we see good design, which is still infrequently, we won't see the components reused without good documentation.*

Ken Brooks comments on the difficulty of anticipating *which* generalization will prove necessary: "I keep having to bend things even on the fifth use of my own personal user-interface library."

Real reuse seems to be just beginning. Jones reports that a few reusable code modules are being offered on the open market at prices between 1 percent and 20 percent of the normal development costs.[27] DeMarco says,

> *I am becoming very discouraged about the whole reuse phenomenon. There is almost a total absence of an existence theorem for reuse. Time has confirmed that there is a* big *expense in making things reusable.*

Yourdon estimates the big expense: "A good rule of thumb is that such reusable components will take twice the effort of a 'one-shot' component."[28] I see that expense as exactly the effort of productizing the component, discussed in Chapter 1. So my estimate of the effort ratio would be threefold.

Clearly we are seeing many forms and varieties of reuse, but not nearly so much of it as we had expected by now. There is still a lot to learn.

Learning Large Vocabularies—A Predictable but Unpredicted Problem for Software Reuse

The higher the level at which one thinks, the more numerous the primitive thought-elements one has to deal with. So programming languages are much more complex than machine languages, and natural languages are more complex still. Higher-level languages have larger vocabularies, more complex syntax, and richer semantics.

As a discipline, we have not pondered the implications of this fact for program reuse. To improve quality and productivity, we want to build programs by composing chunks of debugged function that are substantially higher than statements in programming languages. Therefore, whether we do this by object class libraries or procedure libraries, we must face the fact that we are radically raising the sizes of our programming vocabularies. Vocabulary learning constitutes no small part of the intellectual barrier to reuse.

So today people have class libraries with over 3000 members. Many objects require specification of 10 to 20 parameters and option variables. Anyone programming with that library must learn the syntax (the external interfaces) and the semantics (the detailed functional behavior) of its members if they are to achieve all of the potential reuse.

This task is far from hopeless. Native speakers routinely use vocabularies of over 10,000 words, educated people far more. Somehow we learn the syntax and very subtle semantics. We correctly differentiate among *giant, huge, vast, enormous, mammoth;* people just do not speak of mammoth deserts or vast elephants.

We need research to appropriate for the software reuse problem the large body of knowledge as to how people acquire language. Some of the lessons are immediately obvious:

- People learn in sentence contexts, so we need to publish many examples of composed products, not just libraries of parts.
- People do not memorize anything but spelling. They learn syntax and semantics incrementally, in context, by use.
- People group word composition rules by syntactic classes, not by compatible subsets of objects.

Net on Bullets—Position Unchanged

So we come back to fundamentals. Complexity *is* the business we are in, and complexity is what limits us. R. L. Glass, writing in 1988, accurately summarizes my 1995 views:

> So what, in retrospect, have Parnas and Brooks said to us? That software development is a conceptually tough business. That magic solutions are not just around the corner. That it is time for the practitioner to examine evolutionary improvements rather than to wait—or hope—for revolutionary ones.
>
> Some in the software field find this to be a discouraging picture. They are the ones who still thought breakthroughs were near at hand.
>
> But some of us—those of us crusty enough to think that we are realists—see this as a breath of fresh air. At last, we can focus on something a little more viable than pie in the sky. Now, perhaps, we can get on with the incremental improvements to software productivity that are possible, rather than waiting for the breakthroughs that are not likely to ever come.[29]

18

Propositions of The Mythical Man-Month: *True or False?*

18

Propositions of The Mythical Man-Month: *True or False?*

For brevity is very good,
Where we are, or are not understood.

SAMUEL BUTLER, Hudibras

Brooks asserting a proposition, 1967
Photo by J. Alex Langley for *Fortune* Magazine

Much more is known today about software engineering than was known in 1975. Which of the assertions in the original 1975 edition have been supported by data and experience? Which have been disproved? Which have been obsoleted by the changing world? To help you judge, here in outline form is the essence of the 1975 book—assertions I believed to be true: facts and rule-of-thumb-type generalizations from experience—extracted without change of meaning. (You might ask, "If this is all the original book said, why did it take 177 pages to say it?") Comments in brackets are new.

Most of these propositions are operationally testable. My hope in putting them forth in stark form is to focus readers' thoughts, measurements, and comments.

Chapter 1.   The Tar Pit

1.1   A programming systems product takes about nine times as much effort as the component programs written separately for private use. I estimate that productizing imposes a factor of three; and that designing, integrating, and testing components into a coherent system imposes a factor of three; and that these cost components are essentially independent of each other.

1.2   The craft of programming "gratifies creative longings built deep within us and delights sensibilities we have in common with all men," providing five kinds of joys:
- The joy of making things
- The joy of making things that are useful to other people
- The fascination of fashioning puzzle-like objects of interlocking moving parts
- The joy of always learning, of a nonrepeating task
- The delight of working in a medium so tractable—pure thought-stuff—which nevertheless exists, moves, and works in a way that word-objects do not.

1.3   Likewise the craft has special woes inherent in it.

- Adjusting to the requirement of perfection is the hardest part of learning to program.
- Others set one's objectives and one must depend upon things (especially programs) one cannot control; the authority is not equal to the responsibility.
- This sounds worse than it is: actual authority comes from momentum of accomplishment.
- With any creativity come dreary hours of painstaking labor; programming is no exception.
- The programming project converges more slowly the nearer one gets to the end, whereas one expects it to converge faster as one approaches the end.
- One's product is always threatened with obsolescence before completion. The real tiger is never a match for the paper one, unless real use is wanted.

Chapter 2.   The Mythical Man-Month

2.1   More programming projects have gone awry for lack of calendar time than for all other causes combined.

2.2   Good cooking takes time; some tasks cannot be hurried without spoiling the result.

2.3   All programmers are optimists: "All will go well."

2.4   Because the programmer builds with pure thought-stuff, we expect few difficulties in implementation.

2.5   But our *ideas* themselves are faulty, so we have bugs.

2.6   Our estimating techniques, built around cost-accounting, confuse effort and progress. *The man-month is a fallacious and dangerous myth, for it implies that men and months are interchangeable.*

2.7   Partitioning a task among multiple people occasions extra communication effort—training and intercommunication.

2.8   My rule of thumb is 1/3 of the schedule for design, 1/6 for coding, 1/4 for component testing, and 1/4 for system testing.

2.9 As a discipline, we lack estimating data.

2.10 Because we are uncertain about our scheduling estimates, we often lack the courage to defend them stubbornly against management and customer pressure.

2.11 Brooks's Law: Adding manpower to a late software project makes it later.

2.12 Adding people to a software project increases the total effort necessary in three ways: the work and disruption of repartitioning itself, training the new people, and added intercommunication.

Chapter 3.   The Surgical Team

3.1 Very good professional programmers are *ten times* as productive as poor ones, at same training and two-year experience level. (Sackman, Grant, and Erickson)

3.2 Sackman, Grant, and Erickson's data showed no correlation whatsoever between experience and performance. I doubt the universality of that result.

3.3 A small sharp team is best—as few minds as possible.

3.4 A team of two, with one leader, is often the best use of minds. [Note God's plan for marriage.]

3.5 A small sharp team is too slow for really big systems.

3.6 Most experiences with really large systems show the brute-force approach to scaling up to be costly, slow, inefficient, and to produce systems that are not conceptually integrated.

3.7 A chief-programmer, surgical-team organization offers a way to get the product integrity of few minds and the total productivity of many helpers, with radically reduced communication.

Chapter 4.   Aristocracy, Democracy, and System Design

4.1 "Conceptual integrity is *the* most important consideration in system design."

4.2   "The *ratio* of function to conceptual complexity is the ultimate test of system design," not just the richness of function. [This ratio is a measure of ease of use, valid over both simple and difficult uses.]

4.3   To achieve conceptual integrity, a design must proceed from one mind or a small group of agreeing minds.

4.4   "Separation of architectural effort from implementation is a very powerful way of getting conceptual integration on very large projects." [Small ones, too.]

4.5   "If a system is to have conceptual integrity, someone must control the concepts. That is an aristocracy that needs no apology."

4.6   Discipline is good for art. The external provision of an architecture enhances, not cramps, the creative style of an implementing group.

4.7   A conceptually integrated system is faster to build and to test.

4.8   Much of software architecture, implementation, and realization can proceed in parallel. [Hardware and software design can likewise proceed in parallel.]

Chapter 5.   The Second-System Effect

5.1   Early and continuous communication can give the architect good cost readings and the builder confidence in the design, without blurring the clear division of responsibilities.

5.2   How an architect can successfully influence implementation:

- Remember that the builder has the creative responsibility for implementation; the architect only suggests.
- Always be ready to suggest a way of implementing anything one specifies; be prepared to accept any other equally good way.
- Deal quietly and privately in such suggestions.
- Be ready to forgo credit for suggested improvements.

- Listen to the builder's suggestions for architecture improvements.

5.3   The second is the most dangerous system a person ever designs; the general tendency is to over-design it.

5.4   OS/360 is a good example of the second-system effect. [Windows NT seems to be a 1990s example.]

5.5   Assigning *a priori* values in bytes and microseconds to functions is a worthwhile discipline.

Chapter 6.   Passing the Word

6.1   Even when a design team is large, the results must be reduced to writing by one or two, in order that the mini-decisions be consistent.

6.2   It is important to explicitly define the parts of an architecture that are *not* prescribed as carefully as those that are.

6.3   One needs both a formal definition of a design, for precision, and a prose definition for comprehensibility.

6.4   One of the formal and prose definitions must be standard, and the other derivative. Either definition can serve in either role.

6.5   An implementation, including a simulation, can serve as an architectural definition; such use has formidable disadvantages.

6.6   Direct incorporation is a very clean technique for enforcing an architectural standard in software. [In hardware, too—consider the Mac WIMP interface built into ROM.]

6.7   An architectural "definition will be cleaner and the [architectural] discipline tighter if at least two implementations are built initially."

6.8   It is important to allow telephone interpretations by an architect in response to implementers' queries; it is imperative to log these and publish them. [Electronic mail is now the medium of choice.]

6.9   "The project manager's best friend is his daily adversary, the independent product-testing organization."

Chapter 7.   Why Did the Tower of Babel Fail?

7.1   The Tower of Babel project failed because of lack of *communication* and of its consequent, *organization*.

Communication

7.2   "Schedule disaster, functional misfit, and system bugs all arise because the left hand doesn't know what the right hand is doing." Teams drift apart in assumptions.

7.3   Teams should communicate with one another in as many ways as possible: informally, by regular project meetings with technical briefings, and via a shared formal project workbook. [And by electronic mail.]

Project Workbook

7.4   A project workbook is "not so much a separate document as it is a structure imposed on the documents that the project will be producing anyway."

7.5   "*All* the documents of the project need to be part of this [workbook] structure."

7.6   The workbook structure needs to be designed *carefully* and *early*.

7.7   Properly structuring the on-going documentation from the beginning "molds later writing into segments that fit into that structure" and will improve the product manuals.

7.8   "*Each* team member should see *all* the [workbook] material." [I would now say, each team member *should be able* to see all of it. That is, World-Wide Web pages would suffice.]

7.9   Timely updating is of critical importance.

7.10 The user needs to have attention especially drawn to changes since his last reading, with remarks on their significance.

7.11 The OS/360 Project workbook started with paper and switched to microfiche.

7.12 Today [even in 1975], the shared electronic notebook is a much better, cheaper, and simpler mechanism for achieving all these goals.

7.13   One still has to mark the text with [the functional equivalent of] change bars and revision dates. One still needs a LIFO electronic change summary.

7.14   Parnas argues strongly that the goal of everyone seeing everything is *totally wrong;* parts should be encapsulated so that no one needs to or is allowed to see the internals of any parts other than his own, but should see only the interfaces.

7.15   Parnas's proposal is a recipe for disaster. [*I have been quite convinced otherwise by Parnas, and totally changed my mind.*]

Organization

7.16   The purpose of organization is to reduce the amount of communication and coordination necessary.

7.17   Organization embodies *division of labor* and *specialization of function* in order to obviate communication.

7.18   The conventional tree organization reflects the *authority* structure principle that no person can serve two masters.

7.19   The *communication* structure in an organization is a network, not a tree, so all kinds of special organization mechanisms ("dotted lines") have to be devised to overcome the communication deficiencies of the tree-structured organization.

7.20   Every subproject has two leadership roles to be filled, that of the *producer* and that of the *technical director,* or *architect.* The functions of the two roles are quite distinct and require different talents.

7.21   Any of three relationships among the two roles can be quite effective:

- The producer and director can be the same.
- The producer may be boss, and the director the producer's right-hand person.
- The director may be boss, and the producer the director's right-hand person.

Chapter 8.   Calling the Shot

8.1   One cannot accurately estimate the total effort or schedule
        of a programming project by simply estimating the coding
        time and multiplying by factors for the other parts of the
        task.

8.2   Data for building isolated small systems are not applicable
        to programming systems projects.

8.3   Programming increases goes as a power of program size.

8.4   Some published studies show the exponent to be about
        1.5. [*Boehm's data do not at all agree with this, but vary from
        1.05 to 1.2.*][1]

8.5   Portman's ICL data show full-time programmers applying
        only about 50 percent of their time to programming and
        debugging, versus other overhead-type tasks.

8.6   Aron's IBM data show productivity varying from 1.5 K
        lines of code (KLOC) per man-year to 10 KLOC/man-year
        as a function of the number of interactions among system
        parts.

8.7   Harr's Bell Labs data show productivities on operating-
        systems-type work to run about 0.6 KLOC/man-year and
        on compiler-type work about 2.2 KLOC/man-year for fin-
        ished products.

8.8   Brooks's OS/360 data agrees with Harr's: 0.6–0.8 KLOC/
        man-year on operating systems and 2–3 KLOC/man-year
        on compilers.

8.9   Corbató's MIT Project MULTICS data show productivity
        of 1.2 KLOC/man-year on a mix of operating systems and
        compilers, but these are PL/I lines of code, whereas all the
        other data are assembler lines of code!

8.10   Productivity seems constant in terms of elementary state-
        ments.

8.11   Programming productivity may be increased as much as
        five times when a suitable high-level language is used.

Chapter 9. Ten Pounds in a Five-Pound Sack

9.1 Aside from running time, the *memory space* occupied by a program is a principal cost. This is especially true for operating systems, where much is resident all the time.

9.2 Even so, money spent on memory for program residence may yield very good functional value per dollar, better than other ways of investing in configuration. Program size is not bad; unnecessary size is.

9.3. The software builder must set size targets, control size, and devise size-reduction techniques, just as the hardware builder does for components.

9.4 Size budgets must be explicit not only about resident size but also about the disk accesses occasioned by program fetches.

9.5 Size budgets have to be tied to function assignments; define exactly what a module must do when you specify how big it must be.

9.6 On large teams, subteams tend to suboptimize to meet their own targets rather than think about the total effect on the user. This breakdown in orientation is a major hazard of large projects.

9.7 All during implementation, the system architects must maintain constant vigilance to ensure continued system integrity.

9.8 Fostering a total-system, user-oriented attitude may well be the most important function of the programming manager.

9.9 An early policy decision is to decide how fine-grained the user choice of options will be, since packaging them in clumps saves memory space [and often marketing costs].

9.10 The size of the transient area, hence of the amount of program per disk fetch, is a crucial decision, since performance is a super-linear function of that size. [This whole decision has been obsoleted, first by virtual memory, then by cheap real memory. Users now typically buy enough real memory to hold all the code of major applications.]

9.11   To make good space-time tradeoffs, a team needs to be trained in the programming techniques peculiar to a particular language or machine, especially a new one.

9.12   Programming has a technology, and every project needs a library of standard components.

9.13   Program libraries should have two versions of each component, the quick and the squeezed. [This seems obsolete today.]

9.14   Lean, spare, fast programs are almost always the result of *strategic breakthrough*, rather than tactical cleverness.

9.15   Often such a breakthrough will be a new *algorithm*.

9.16   More often, the breakthrough will come from redoing the *representation* of the data or tables. *Representation is the essence of programming.*

Chapter 10.   The Documentary Hypothesis

10.1   "The hypothesis: Amid a wash of paper, a small number of documents become the critical pivots around which every project's management revolves. These are the manager's chief personal tools."

10.2   For a computer development project, the critical documents are the objectives, manual, schedule, budget, organization chart, floorspace allocation, and the estimate, forecast, and prices of the machine itself.

10.3   For a university department, the critical documents are similar: the objectives, degree requirements, course descriptions, research proposals, class schedule and teaching plan, budget, floorspace allocation, and assignments of staff and graduate assistants.

10.4   For a software project, the needs are the same: the objectives, user manual, internals documentation, schedule, budget, organization chart, and floorspace allocation.

10.5   Even on a small project, therefore, the manager should from the beginning formalize such a set of documents.

10.6   Preparing each document of this small set focuses thought and crystallizes discussion. The act of writing requires hundreds of mini-decisions, and it is the existence of these that distinguish clear, exact policies from fuzzy ones.

10.7   Maintaining each critical document provides a status surveillance and warning mechanism.

10.8   Each document itself serves as a checklist and a database.

10.9   The project manager's fundamental job is to keep everybody going in the same direction.

10.10   The project manager's chief daily task is communication, not decision-making; the documents communicate the plans and decisions to the whole team.

10.11   Only a small part of a technical project manager's time—perhaps 20 percent—is spent on tasks where he needs information from outside his head.

10.12   For this reason, the touted market concept of a "management total-information system" to support executives is not based on a valid model of executive behavior.

Chapter 11.   Plan to Throw One Away

11.1   Chemical engineers have learned not to take a process from the lab bench to the factory in one step, but to build a *pilot plant* to give experience in scaling quantities up and operating in nonprotective environments.

11.2   This intermediate step is equally necessary for programming products, but software engineers do not yet routinely field-test a pilot system before undertaking to deliver the real product. [This has now become common practice, with a beta version. This is not the same as a prototype with limited function, an alpha version, which I would also advocate.]

11.3   For most projects, the first system built is barely usable: too slow, too big, too hard to use, or all three.

11.4 The discard and redesign may be done in one lump, or piece-by-piece, but *it will be done.*

11.5 Delivering the first system, the throwaway, to users will buy time, but only at the cost of agony for the user, distraction for the builders supporting it while they do the redesign, and a bad reputation for the product that will be hard to live down.

11.6 Hence, *plan to throw one away; you will, anyhow.*

11.7 "The programmer delivers satisfaction of a user need rather than any tangible product." (Cosgrove)

11.8 Both the actual need and the user's perception of that need will *change* as programs are built, tested, and used.

11.9 The tractability and the invisibility of the software product expose its builders (exceptionally) to perpetual changes in requirements.

11.10 Some valid changes in objectives (and in development strategies) are inevitable, and it is better to be prepared for them than to assume that they will not come.

11.11 The techniques for planning a software product for change, especially structured programming with careful module interface documentation, are well known but not uniformly practiced. It also helps to use table-driven techniques wherever possible. [Modern memory costs and sizes make such techniques better and better.]

11.12 Use high-level language, compile-time operations, incorporations of declarations by reference, and self-documenting techniques to reduce errors induced by change.

11.13 Quantify changes into well-defined numbered versions. [Now standard practice.]

Plan the Organization for Change

11.14 Programmer reluctance to document designs comes not so much from laziness as from the hesitancy to undertake defense of decisions that the designer knows are tentative. (Cosgrove)

11.15 Structuring an organization for change is much harder than designing a system for change.

11.16 The project boss must work at keeping the managers and the technical people as interchangeable as their talents allow; in particular, one wants to be able to move people easily between technical and managerial roles.

11.17 The barriers to effective dual-ladder organization are sociological, and they must be fought with constant vigilance and energy.

11.18 It is easy to establish corresponding salary scales for the corresponding rungs on a dual ladder, but it requires strong proactive measures to give them corresponding prestige: equal offices, equal support services, over-compensating management actions.

11.19 Organizing as a surgical team is a radical attack on all aspects of this problem. It is really the long-run answer to the problem of flexible organization.

Two Steps Forward and One Step Back— Program Maintenance

11.20 Program maintenance is fundamentally different from hardware maintenance; it consists chiefly of changes that repair design defects, add incremental function, or adapt to changes in the use environment or configuration.

11.21 The total lifetime cost of maintaining a widely used program is typically 40 percent or more of the cost of developing it.

11.22 Maintenance cost is strongly affected by the number of users. More users find more bugs.

11.23 Campbell points out an interesting drop-and-climb curve in bugs per month over a product's life.

11.24 Fixing a defect has a substantial (20 to 50 percent) chance of introducing another.

11.25 After each fix, one must run the entire bank of test cases previously run against a system to ensure that it has not been damaged in an obscure way.

11.26 Methods of designing programs so as to eliminate or at least illuminate side effects can have an immense payoff in maintenance costs.

11.27 So can methods of implementing designs with fewer people, fewer interfaces, and fewer bugs.

One Step Forward and One Step Back—System Entropy Rises over Lifetime

11.28 Lehman and Belady find that the total number of modules increases linearly with the release number of a large operating system (OS/360), but that the number of modules affected increases exponentially with the release number.

11.29 All repairs tend to destroy structure, to increase the entropy and disorder of a system. Even the most skillful program maintenance only delays the program's subsidence into unfixable chaos, from which there has to be a ground-up redesign. [Many of the real needs for upgrading a program, such as performance, especially attack its internal structural boundaries. Often the original boundaries occasioned the deficiencies that surface later.]

Chapter 12.   Sharp Tools

12.1 The manager of a project needs to establish a philosophy and set aside resources for the building of common tools, and at the same time to recognize the need for personalized tools.

12.2 Teams building operating systems need a target machine of their own on which to debug; it needs maximum memory rather than maximum speed, and a system programmer to keep the standard software current and serviceable.

12.3 The debugging machine, or its software, also needs to be instrumented, so that counts and measurements of all kinds of program parameters can be automatically made.

12.4   The requirement for target machine use has a peculiar growth curve: low activity followed by explosive growth, then leveling off.

12.5   System debugging, like astronomy, has always been done chiefly at night.

12.6   Allocating substantial blocks of target machine time to one subteam at a time proved the best way to schedule, much better than interleaving subteam use, despite theory.

12.7   This preferred method of scheduling scarce computers by blocks has survived 20 years [in 1975] of technology change because it is most productive. [It still is, in 1995].

12.8   If a target computer is new, one needs a logical simulator for it. One gets it *sooner,* and it provides a *dependable* debugging vehicle even after one has a real machine.

12.9   A master program library should be divided into (1) a set of individual playpens, (2) a system integration sublibrary, currently under system test, and (3) a released version. Formal separation and progression gives control.

12.10   The tool that saves the most labor in a programming project is probably a text-editing system.

12.11   Voluminosity in system documentation does indeed introduce a new kind of incomprehensibility [see Unix, for example], but it is far preferable to the severe underdocumentation that is so common.

12.12   Build a performance simulator, outside in, top down. Start it very early. Listen when it speaks.

High-Level Language

12.13   Only sloth and inertia prevent the universal adoption of high-level language and interactive programming. [And today they have been adopted universally.]

12.14   High-level language improves not only productivity but also debugging; fewer bugs and easier to find.

12.15   The classical objections of function, object-code space, and object-code speed have been made obsolete by the advance of language and compiler technology.

12.16 The only reasonable candidate for system programming today is PL/I. [No longer true.]

Interactive Programming

12.17 Interactive systems will never displace batch systems for some applications. [Still true.]

12.18 Debugging is the hard and slow part of system programming, and slow turnaround is the bane of debugging.

12.19 Limited evidence shows that interactive programming at least doubles productivity in system programming.

Chapter 13.   The Whole and the Parts

13.1 The detailed, painstaking architectural effort implied in Chapters 4, 5, and 6 not only makes a product easier to use, it makes it easier to build and reduces the number of system bugs that have to be found.

13.2 Vyssotsky says "Many, many failures concern exactly those aspects that were never quite specified."

13.3 Long before any code itself, the specification must be handed to an outside testing group to be scrutinized for completeness and clarity. The developers themselves cannot do this. (Vyssotsky)

13.4 "Wirth's top-down design [by stepwise refinement] is the most important new programming formalization of the [1965–1975] decade."

13.5 Wirth advocates using as high-level a notation as possible on each step.

13.6 A good top-down design avoids bugs in four ways.

13.7 Sometimes one has to go back, scrap a high level, and start over.

13.8 Structured programming, designing programs whose control structures consist only of a specified set that govern blocks of code (versus miscellaneous branching), is a sound way to avoid bugs and is the right way to think.

13.9 Gold's experimental results show three times as much progress is made in the first interaction of an interactive debugging session as on subsequent interactions. It still pays to plan debugging carefully before signing on. [I think it *still* does, in 1995.]

13.10 I find that proper use of a good [quick response interactive debugging] system requires two hours at the desk for each two-hour session on the machine: one hour in sweeping up and documenting after the session and one in planning changes and tests for the next time.

13.11 System debugging (in contrast to component debugging) will take longer than one expects.

13.12 The difficulty of system debugging justifies a thoroughly systematic and planned approach.

13.13 One should begin system debugging only after the pieces seem to work (versus-bolt-it-together-and-try in order to smoke out the interface bugs; and versus starting system debugging when the component bugs are fully known but not fixed.) [This is especially true for teams.]

13.14 It is worthwhile to build lots of debugging scaffolding and test code, perhaps even 50 percent as much as the product being debugged.

13.15 One must control and document changes and versions, with team members working in playpen copies.

13.16 Add one component at a time during system debugging.

13.17 Lehman and Belady offer evidence the change quanta should be large and infrequent or else very small and frequent. The latter is more subject to instability. [A Microsoft team makes small frequent quanta work. The growing system is rebuilt every night.]

Chapter 14. Hatching a Catastrophe

14.1 "How does a project get to be a year late? . . . One day at a time."

14.2   Day-by-day schedule slippage is harder to recognize, harder to prevent, and harder to make up than calamities.

14.3   The first step in controlling a big project on a tight schedule is to *have* a schedule, made up of milestones and dates for them.

14.4   Milestones must be concrete, specific, measurable events defined with knife-edge sharpness.

14.5   A programmer will rarely lie about milestone progress, if the milestone is so sharp he can't deceive himself.

14.6   Studies of estimating behavior by government contractors on large projects show that activity time estimates revised carefully every two weeks do not significantly change as the start time approaches, that during the activity *over*estimates come steadily down; and that *under*estimates do not change until about three weeks before scheduled completion.

14.7   Chronic schedule slippage is a morale-killer. [Jim McCarthy of Microsoft says, "If you miss one deadline, make sure you make the next one."[2]]

14.8   *Hustle* is essential for great programming teams, just as for great baseball teams.

14.9   There is no substitute for a critical-path schedule to enable one to tell which slips matter how much.

14.10 The preparation of a critical-path chart is the most valuable part of its use, since laying out the network, identifying the dependencies, and estimating the segments force a great deal of very specific planning very early in a project.

14.11 The first chart is always terrible, and one invents and invents in making the next one.

14.12 A critical path chart answers the demoralizing excuse, "The other piece is late, anyhow."

14.13 Every boss needs both exception information that requires action and a status picture for education and distant early warning.

14.14 Getting the status is hard, since subordinate managers have every reason not to share it.

14.15 By bad action, a boss can guarantee to squelch full status disclosure; conversely, carefully separating status reports and accepting them without panic or preemption will encourage honest reporting.

14.16 One must have review techniques by which true status becomes known to all players. For this purpose a milestone schedule and completion document is the key.

14.17 Vyssotsky: "I have found it handy to carry both 'scheduled' (boss's dates) and 'estimated' (lowest-level manager's dates) dates in the milestone report. The project manager has to keep his fingers off the estimated dates."

14.18 A small *Plans and Controls* team that maintains the milestone report is invaluable for a large project.

Chapter 15. The Other Face

15.1 For the program product, the other face to the user, the documentation, is fully as important as the face to the machine.

15.2 Even for the most private of programs, prose documentation is necessary, for memory will fail the user-author.

15.3 Teachers and managers have by and large failed to instill in programmers an attitude about documentation that will inspire for a lifetime, overcoming sloth and schedule pressure.

15.4 This failure is not due so much to lack of zeal or eloquence as to a failure to show *how* to document effectively and economically.

15.5 Most documentation fails in giving too little *overview.* Stand way back and zoom in slowly.

15.6 The critical user documentation should be drafted before the program is built, for it embodies basic planning decisions. It should describe nine things (see the chapter).

15.7 A program should be shipped with a few test cases, some for valid input data, some for borderline input data, and some for clearly invalid input data.

15.8   Documentation of program internals, for the person who must modify it, also demands a prose overview, which should contain five kinds of things (see the chapter).

15.9   The flow chart is a most thoroughly oversold piece of program documentation; the detailed blow-by-blow flow chart is a nuisance, obsoleted by *written* high-level languages. (A flow chart is a *diagrammed* high-level language.)

15.10   Few programs need more than a one-page flow chart, if that. [MILSPEC documentation requirements are really wrong on this point.]

15.11   One does indeed need a program structure graph, which does not need the ANSI flow-charting standards.

15.12   To keep documentation maintained, it is crucial that it be incorporated in the source program, rather than kept as a separate document.

15.13   Three notions are key to minimizing the documentation burden:
   • Use parts of the program that have to be there anyway, such as names and declarations, to carry as much of the documentation as possible.
   • Use space and format to show subordination and nesting and to improve readability.
   • Insert the necessary prose documentation into the program as paragraphs of comment, especially as module headers.

15.14   In documentation for use by program modifiers, tell *why* things are like they are, rather than merely how they are. *Purpose* is the key to understanding; even high-level language syntax does not at all convey purpose.

15.15   Self-documenting programming techniques find their greatest use and power in high-level languages used with on-line systems, which are the tools one *should* be using.

Original Epilogue

E.1   Software systems are perhaps the most intricate and complex (in terms of number of distinct kinds of parts) of the things humanity makes.

E.2   The tar pit of software engineering will continue to be sticky for a long time to come.

19
The Mythical Man-Month
after 20 *Years*

19

The Mythical Man-Month after 20 Years

I know no way of judging the future but by the past.

PATRICK HENRY

You can never plan the future by the past.

EDMUND BURKE

Shooting the Rapids
The Bettman Archive

Why Is There a Twentieth Anniversary Edition?

The plane droned through the night toward LaGuardia. Clouds and darkness veiled all interesting sights. The document I was studying was pedestrian. I was not, however, bored. The stranger sitting next to me was reading *The Mythical Man-Month*, and I was waiting to see if by word or sign he would react. Finally as we taxied toward the gate, I could wait no longer:

"How is that book? Do you recommend it?"

"Hmph! Nothing in it I didn't know already."

I decided not to introduce myself.

Why has *The Mythical Man-Month* persisted? Why is it still seen to be relevant to software practice today? Why does it have a readership outside the software engineering community, generating reviews, citations, and correspondence from lawyers, doctors, psychologists, sociologists, as well as from software people? How can a book written 20 years ago about a software-building experience 30 years ago still be relevant, much less useful?

One explanation sometimes heard is that the software development discipline has not advanced normally or properly. This view is often supported by contrasting computer software development productivity with computer hardware manufacturing productivity, which has multiplied at least a thousand-fold over the two decades. As Chapter 16 explains, the anomaly is not that software has been so slow in its progress but rather that computer technology has exploded in a fashion unmatched in human history. By and large this comes from the gradual transition of computer manufacturing from an assembly industry to a process industry, from labor-intensive to capital-intensive manufacturing. Hardware and software development, in contrast to manufacturing, remain inherently labor-intensive.

A second explanation often advanced is that *The Mythical Man-Month* is only incidentally about software but primarily about how people in teams make things. There is surely some truth in this; the preface to the 1975 edition says that managing a software project is more like other management than most programmers initially believe. I still believe that to be true. Human history is a drama in which the stories stay the same, the scripts of those stories change slowly with evolving cultures, and the stage settings change all the time. So it is that we see our twentieth-century selves mirrored in Shakespeare, Homer, and the Bible. So to the extent *The MM-M* is about people and teams, obsolescence should be slow.

Whatever the reason, readers continue to buy the book, and they continue to send me much-appreciated comments. Nowadays I am often asked, "What do you now think was wrong when written? What is now obsolete? What is really new in the software engineering world?" These quite distinct questions are all fair, and I shall address them as best I can. Not in that order, however, but in clusters of topics. First, let us consider what was right when written, and still is.

The Central Argument: Conceptual Integrity and the Architect

Conceptual integrity.   A clean, elegant programming product must present to each of its users a coherent mental model of the application, of strategies for doing the application, and of the user-interface tactics to be used in specifying actions and parameters. The conceptual integrity of the product, as perceived by the user, is the most important factor in ease of use. (There are other factors, of course. The Macintosh's uniformity of user interface across all applications is an important example. Moreover, it is possible to construct coherent interfaces that are nevertheless quite awkward. Consider MS-DOS.)

There are many examples of elegant software products designed by a single mind, or by a pair. Most purely intellectual works such as books or musical compositions are so produced. Product-development processes in many industries cannot, however, afford this straightforward approach to conceptual integrity. Competitive pressures force urgency; in many modern technologies the end product is quite complex, and the design inherently requires many man-months of effort. Software products are both complex and fiercely competitive in schedule.

Any product that is sufficiently big or urgent to require the effort of many minds thus encounters a peculiar difficulty: the result must be conceptually coherent to the single mind of the user and at the same time designed by many minds. How does one organize design efforts so as to achieve such conceptual integrity? This is the central question addressed by *The MM-M.* One of its theses is that managing large programming projects is qualitatively different from managing small ones, just because of the number of minds involved. Deliberate, and even heroic, management actions are necessary to achieve coherence.

The architect.   I argue in Chapters 4 through 7 that the most important action is the commissioning of some one mind to be the product's *architect,* who is responsible for the conceptual integrity of all aspects of the product perceivable by the user. The architect forms and owns the public mental model of the product that will be used to explain its use to the user. This includes the detailed specification of all of its function and the means for invoking and controlling it. The architect is also the user's agent, knowledgeably representing the user's interest in the inevitable tradeoffs among function, performance, size, cost, and schedule. This role is a full-time job, and only on the smallest teams can it be combined with that of the team manager. The architect is like the director and the manager like the producer of a motion picture.

Separation of architecture from implementation and realization.   To make the architect's crucial task even conceivable, it is necessary to separate the architecture, the definition of the product as perceivable by the user, from its implementation. Architecture versus implementation defines a clean boundary between parts of the design task, and there is plenty of work on each side of it.

Recursion of architects.   For quite large products, one mind cannot do all of the architecture, even after all implementation concerns have been split off. So it is necessary for the system master architect to partition the system into subsystems. The subsystem boundaries must be at those places where interfaces between the subsystems are minimal and easiest to define rigorously. Then each piece will have its own architect, who must report to the system master architect with respect to the architecture. Clearly this process can proceed recursively as required.

Today I am more convinced than ever.   Conceptual integrity *is* central to product quality. Having a system architect *is* the most important single step toward conceptual integrity. These principles are by no means limited to software systems, but to the design of any complex construct, whether a computer, an airplane, a Strategic Defense Initiative, a Global Positioning System. After teaching a software engineering laboratory more than 20 times, I came to insist that student teams as small as four people choose a manager and a separate architect. Defining distinct roles in such small teams may be a little extreme, but I have observed it to work well and to contribute to design success even for small teams.

The Second-System Effect: Featuritis and Frequency-Guessing

Designing for large user sets.   One of the consequences of the personal computer revolution is that increasingly, at least in the business data processing community, off-the-shelf packages are replacing custom applications. Moreover, standard software packages sell hundreds of thousands of copies, or even millions. System architects for machine-vendor-supplied software have always had to design for a large, amorphous user set rather than for a single, definable application in one company. Many, many system architects now face this task.

Paradoxically, it is much more difficult to design a general-purpose tool than it is to design a special-purpose tool, precisely because one has to assign weights to the differing needs of the diverse users.

Featuritis.   The besetting temptation for the architect of a general purpose tool such as a spreadsheet or a word processor is to overload the product with features of marginal utility, at the expense of performance and even of ease of use. The appeal of proposed features is evident at the outset; the performance penalty is evident only as system testing proceeds. The loss of ease of use sneaks up insidiously, as features are added in little increments, and the manuals wax fatter and fatter.[1]

For mass-market products that survive and evolve through many generations, the temptation is especially strong. Millions of customers request hundreds of features; any request is itself evidence that "the market demands it." Frequently, the original system architect has gone on to greater glories, and the architecture is in the hands of people with less experience at representing the user's overall interest in balance. A recent review of Microsoft Word 6.0 says "Word 6.0 packs in features; update slowed by baggage. . . . Word 6.0 is also big and slow." It notes with dismay that Word 6.0 requires 4 MB of RAM, and goes on to say that the rich added function means that "even a Macintosh IIfx [is] just barely up to the Word 6 task".[2]

Defining the user set.   The larger and more amorphous the user set, the more necessary it is to define it explicitly if one is to achieve conceptual integrity. Each member of the design team will surely have an implicit mental image of the users, and each designer's image will be different. Since an architect's image of the user consciously or subconsciously affects every architectural decision, it is essential for a design team to arrive at a single shared image. And that requires writing down the attributes of the expected user set, including:

- Who they are
- What they need

- What they think they need
- What they want

Frequencies.   For any software product, any of the attributes of the user set is in fact a distribution, with many possible values, each with its own frequency. How is the architect to arrive at these frequencies? Surveying this ill-defined population is a dubious and costly proposition.[3] Over the years I have become convinced that an architect should *guess,* or, if you prefer, *postulate,* a complete set of attributes and values with their frequencies, in order to develop a complete, explicit, and shared description of the user set.

Many benefits flow from this unlikely procedure. First, the process of carefully guessing the frequencies will cause the architect to think very carefully about the expected user set. Second, writing the frequencies down will subject them to debate, which will illuminate all the participants and bring to the surface the differences in the user images that the several designers carry. Third, enumerating the frequencies explicitly helps everyone recognize which decisions depend upon which user set properties. Even this sort of informal sensitivity analysis is valuable. When it develops that very important decisions are hinging on some particular guess, then it is worth the cost to establish better estimates for that value. (The gIBIS system developed by Jeff Conklin provides a tool for formally and accurately tracking design decisions and documenting the reasons for each.[4] I have not had opportunity to use it, but I think it would be very helpful.)

To summarize: write down explicit guesses for the attributes of the user set. *It is far better to be explicit and wrong than to be vague.*

What about the "Second-System Effect"?   A perceptive student remarked that *The Mythical Man-Month* recommended a recipe for disaster: Plan to deliver the second version of any new system (Chapter 11), which Chapter 5 characterizes as the most dangerous system one ever designs. I had to grant him a "gotcha."

The contradiction is more linguistic than real. The "second" system described in Chapter 5 is the second system fielded, the follow-on system that invites added function and frills. The "second" system in Chapter 11 is the second try at building what should be the first system to be fielded. It is built under all the schedule, talent, and ignorance constraints that characterize new projects—the constraints that exert a slimness discipline.

The Triumph of the WIMP Interface

One of the most impressive developments in software during the past two decades has been the triumph of the Windows, Icons, Menus, Pointing interface—or WIMP for short. It is today so familiar as to need no description. This concept was first publicly displayed by Doug Englebart and his team from the Stanford Research Institute at the Western Joint Computer Conference of 1968.[5] From there the ideas went to Xerox Palo Alto Research Center, where they emerged in the Alto personal workstation developed by Bob Taylor and team. They were picked up by Steve Jobs for the Apple Lisa, a computer too slow to carry its exciting ease-of-use concepts. These concepts Jobs then embodied in the commercially successful Apple Macintosh in 1985. They were later adopted in Microsoft Windows for the IBM PC and compatibles. The Mac version will be my example.[6]

Conceptual integrity via a metaphor. The WIMP is a superb example of a user interface that has conceptual integrity, achieved by the adoption of a familiar mental model, the desktop metaphor, and its careful consistent extension to exploit a computer graphics implementation. For example, the costly but proper decision to overlay windows instead of tiling them follows directly from the metaphor. The ability to size and shape windows is a consistent extension that gives the user the new powers enabled by the computer graphics medium. Papers on a desktop cannot be so readily sized and shaped. Dragging and dropping follow directly from the metaphor; selecting icons by pointing with a cursor is a direct analog of picking things with the hand. Icons and nested folders are faithful analogs of desktop documents; so is the trash can. The concepts of cutting, copying, and pasting faithfully mirror the things we used to do with documents on desktops. So faithfully is the metaphor followed and so consistent is its extension that new users are positively jarred by the notion of dragging a diskette's icon to the trash to eject the disk. Were the interface not almost uniformly consistent, that (pretty bad) inconsistency would not grate so much.

Where is the WIMP interface forced to go far beyond the desktop metaphor? Most notably in two respects: menus and one-handedness. When working with a real desktop, one *does* actions to documents, rather than telling someone or something to do them. And when one does tell someone to do an action, one usually generates, rather than selects, the oral or written imperative verb commands: "Please file this." "Please find the earlier correspondence." "Please send this to Mary to handle."

Alas, the reliable interpretation of free-form generated English commands is beyond the present state of the art, whether commands are written or spoken. So the interface designers were two steps removed from direct user action on documents. They wisely picked up from the usual desktop its one example of command selection—the printed buck slip, on which the user selects from among a constrained menu of commands whose semantics are standardized. This idea they extended to a horizontal menu of vertical pull-down submenus.

Command utterances and the two-cursor problem. Commands are imperative sentences; they always have a verb and usually have a direct object. For any action, one needs to specify a verb and a noun. The pointing metaphor says, to specify two things at a time, have two distinguished cursors on the screen, each driven by a separate mouse—one in the right hand and one in the left. After all, on a physical desktop we normally work with both hands. (But, one hand is often holding things fixed in place, which happens by default on the computer desktop.) The mind is certainly capable of two-handed operation; we regularly use two hands in typing, driving, cooking. Alas, providing one mouse was already a big step forward for personal computer makers; no commercial system accommodates two simultaneous mouse-cursor actions, one driven with each hand.[7]

The interface designers accepted reality and designed for one mouse, adopting the syntactic convention that one points out (*selects*) the noun first. One points at the verb, a menu item. This really gives away a lot of ease-of-use. As I watch users, or videotapes of users, or computer tracings of cursor movements, I am immediately struck that one cursor is having to do the work of two: pick an object in the desktop part of the window; pick a verb in the menu portion; find or re-find an object in the desktop; again pull down a menu (often the same one) and pick a verb. Back and forth, back and forth the cursor goes, from data-space to menu-space, each time discarding the useful information as to where it was last time it was in this space—altogether, an inefficient process.

A brilliant solution.   Even if the electronics and software could readily handle two simultaneously active cursors, there are space-layout difficulties. The desktop in the WIMP metaphor really includes a typewriter, and one must accommodate its real keyboard in physical space on the real desktop. A keyboard plus two mouse-pads uses a lot of the arm's-reach real estate. Well, the problem of the keyboard can be turned into an opportunity—why not enable efficient two-handed operation by using one hand on the keyboard to specify verbs and the other hand on a mouse to pick nouns. Now the cursor stays in the data space, exploiting the high locality of successive noun picks. Real efficiency, real user power.

User power versus ease of use.   That solution, however, gives away the thing that makes menus so easy to use for novices—menus present the alternative verbs valid at any particular state. We can buy a package, bring it home, and start using it without consulting the manual, merely by knowing what we bought it for, and experimenting with the different menu verbs.

One of the hardest issues facing software architects is exactly how to balance user power versus ease of use. Do they design for simple operation for the novice or the occasional user, or for efficient power for the professional user? The ideal answer is to provide both, in a conceptually coherent way—that is achieved in the WIMP interface. The high-frequency menu verbs each have single-key + command-key equivalents, mostly chosen so that they can easily be struck as a single chord with the left hand. On the Mac, for example, the command key (⌘) is just below the Z and X keys; therefore the highest-frequency operations are encoded as ⌘z, ⌘x, ⌘c, ⌘v, ⌘s.

Incremental transition from novice to power user.   This dual system for specifying command verbs not only meets the low-learning-effort needs of the novice and the efficiency needs of the power user, it provides for each user to make a smooth transition between modes. The letter encodings, called *short cuts*, are shown on the menus beside the verbs, so that a user in doubt can pull down the menu to check the letter equivalent, instead of just picking the menu item. Each novice learns first the short cuts for his own high-frequency operations. Any short cut he is doubtful about he can try, since ⌘z will undo any single mistake. Alternatively, he can check the menu to see what commands are valid. Novices will pull lots of menus; power users very few; and in-between users will only occasionally need to pick from a menu, since each will know the few short-cuts that make up most of his own operations. Most of us software designers are too familiar with this interface to appreciate fully its elegance and power.

The success of direct incorporation as a device for enforcing architecture.   The Mac interface is remarkable in yet another way. Without coercion, its designers have made it a standard interface across applications, including the vast majority that are written by third parties. So the user gains conceptual coherence at the interface level not only within the software furnished with the machine but across all applications.

This feat the Mac designers accomplished by building the interface into the read-only memory, so that it is easier and faster for developers to use it than to build their own idiosyncratic interfaces. These natural incentives for uniformity prevailed widely enough to establish a *de facto* standard. The natural incentives were helped by a total management commitment and a lot of persuasion by Apple. The independent reviewers in the product magazines, recognizing the immense value of cross-application conceptual integrity, have also supplemented the natural incentives by mercilessly criticizing products that do not conform.

This is a superb example of the technique, recommended in Chapter 6, of achieving uniformity by encouraging others to directly incorporate one's code into their products, rather than attempting to have them build their own software to one's specifications.

The fate of WIMP: Obsolescence.   Despite its excellencies, I expect the WIMP interface to be a historical relic in a generation. Pointing will still be the way to express nouns as we command our machines; speech is surely the right way to express the verbs. Tools such as Voice Navigator for the Mac and Dragon for the PC already provide this capability.

Don't Build One to Throw Away—The Waterfall Model Is Wrong!

The unforgettable picture of Galloping Gertie, the Tacoma Narrows Bridge, opens Chapter 11, which radically recommends:

"Plan to throw one away; you will, anyhow." This I now perceive to be wrong, not because it is too radical, but because it is too simplistic.

The biggest mistake in the "Build one to throw away" concept is that it implicitly assumes the classical sequential or waterfall model of software construction. The model derives from a Gantt chart layout of a staged process, and it is often drawn as in Figure 19.1. Winton Royce improved the sequential model in a classic 1970 paper by providing for

- Some feedback from a stage to its predecessors
- Limiting the feedback to the immediately preceding stage only, so as to contain the cost and schedule delay it occasions.

He preceded *The MM-M* in advising builders to "build it twice."[8] Chapter 11 is not the only one tainted by the sequential waterfall model; it runs through the book, beginning with the scheduling rule in Chapter 2. That rule-of-thumb allocates 1/3 of the schedule to planning, 1/6 to coding, 1/4 to component test, and 1/4 to system test.

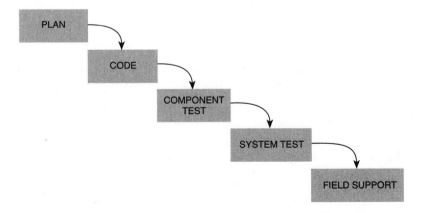

Fig. 19.1 Waterfall model of software construction

The basic fallacy of the waterfall model is that it assumes a project goes through the process *once*, that the architecture is excellent and easy to use, the implementation design is sound, and the realization is fixable as testing proceeds. Another way of saying it is that the waterfall model assumes the mistakes will all be in the realization, and thus that their repair can be smoothly interspersed with component and system testing.

"Plan to throw one away" does indeed attack this fallacy head on. It is not the diagnosis that is wrong; it is the remedy. Now I did suggest that one might discard and redesign the first system piece by piece, rather than in one lump. This is fine so far as it goes, but it fails to get at the root of the problem. The waterfall model puts system test, and therefore by implication *user* testing, at the end of the construction process. Thus one can find impossible awkwardnesses for users, or unacceptable performance, or dangerous susceptibility to user error or malice, only after investing in full construction. To be sure, the Alpha test scrutiny of the specifications aims to find such flaws early, but there is no substitute for hands-on users.

The second fallacy of the waterfall model is that it assumes one builds a whole system at once, combining the pieces for an end-to-end system test after all of the implementation design, most of the coding, and much of the component testing has been done.

The waterfall model, which was the way most people thought about software projects in 1975, unfortunately got enshrined into DOD-STD-2167, the Department of Defense specification for all military software. This ensured its survival well past the time when most thoughtful practitioners had recognized its inadequacy and abandoned it. Fortunately, the DoD has since begun to see the light.[9]

There has to be upstream movement.   Like the energetic salmon in the chapter-opening picture, experience and ideas from each downstream part of the construction process must leap upstream, sometimes more than one stage, and affect the upstream activity.

Designing the implementation will show that some architectural features cripple performance; so the architecture has to be reworked. Coding the realization will show some functions to balloon space requirements; so there may have to be changes to architecture and implementation.

One may well, therefore, iterate through two or more architecture–implementation design cycles before realizing anything as code.

An Incremental-Build Model Is Better— Progressive Refinement

Building an end-to-end skeleton system
Harlan Mills, working in a real-time system environment, early advocated that we should build the basic polling loop of a real-time system, with subroutine calls (*stubs*) for all the functions (Fig. 19.2), but only null subroutines. Compile it; test it. It goes round and round, doing literally nothing, but doing it correctly.[10]

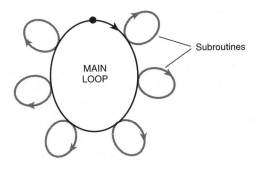

Fig. 19.2

Next, we flesh out a (perhaps primitive) input module and an output module. Voilá! A running system that does something, however dull. Now, function by function, we incrementally build and add modules. *At every stage we have a running system.* If we are diligent, we have at every stage a debugged, tested system. (As the system grows, so does the burden of regression-testing each new module against all the previous test cases.)

After every function works at a primitive level, we refine or rewrite first one module and then another, incrementally *growing* the system. Sometimes, to be sure, we have to change the original driving loop, and or even its module interfaces.

Since we have a working system at all times

- we can begin user testing very early, and
- we can adopt a build-to-budget strategy that protects absolutely against schedule or budget overruns (at the cost of possible functional shortfall).

For some 22 years, I taught the software engineering laboratory at the University of North Carolina, sometimes jointly with David Parnas. In this course, teams of usually four students built in one semester some real software application system. About halfway through those years, I switched to teaching incremental development. I was stunned by the electrifying effect on team morale of that first picture on the screen, that first running system.

Parnas Families
David Parnas has been a major thought leader in software engineering during this whole 20-year period. Everyone is familiar with his information-hiding concept. Rather less familiar, but very important, is Parnas's concept of designing a software product as a *family* of related products.[11] He urges the designer to anticipate both lateral extensions and succeeding versions of

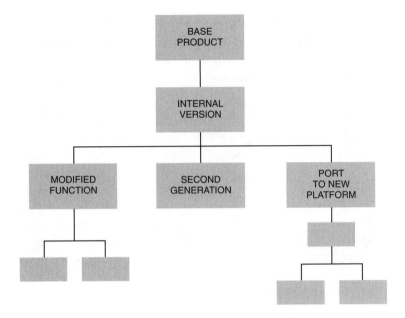

Fig. 19.3

a product, and to define their function or platform differences so as to construct a family tree of related products (Fig 19.3).

The trick in the design of such a tree is to put near its root those design decisions that are less likely to change.

Such a design strategy maximizes the re-use of modules. More important, the same strategy can be broadened to include not only deliverable products but also the successive intermediate versions created in an incremental-build strategy. The product then grows through its intermediate stages with minimum backtracking.

Microsoft's "Build Every Night" Approach

James McCarthy described to me a product process used by his team and others at Microsoft. It is incremental growth carried to a logical conclusion. He says,

> *After we first ship, we will be shipping later versions that add more function to an existing, running product. Why should the initial building process be different? Beginning at the time of our first milestone [where the march to first ship has three intermediate milestones] we rebuild the developing system every night [and run the test cases]. The build cycle becomes the heartbeat of the project. Every day one or more of the programmer-tester teams check in modules with new functions. After every build, we have a running system. If the build breaks, we stop the whole process until the trouble is found and fixed. At all times everybody on the team knows the status.*
>
> *It is really hard. You have to devote lots of resources, but it is a disciplined process, a tracked and known process. It gives the team credibility to itself. Your credibility determines your morale, your emotional state.*

Software builders in other organizations are surprised, even shocked, by this process. One says, "I've made it a practice to build every week, but I think it would be too much work to build every night." And that may be true. Bell Northern Research, for example, rebuilds its 12-million-line system every week.

Incremental-Build and Rapid Prototyping

Since an incremental development process enables early testing with real users, what is the difference between that and rapid prototyping? It seems to me that the two are related but separate. One can have either without the other.

Harel usefully defines a prototype as

> *[A version of a program that] reflects only the design decisions made in the process of preparing the conceptual model, and not decisions driven by implementation concerns.*[12]

It is possible to build a prototype that is not at all part of a product growing toward shipment. For example, one may build an interface prototype that has no real program function behind it, merely the finite-state machine that makes it appear to go through its paces. One can even prototype and test interfaces by the Wizard-of-Oz technique, with a concealed human simulating the system's responses. Such prototyping can be very useful for getting early user feedback, but it is quite apart from testing a product growing toward shipment.

Similarly, implementers may well undertake to build a vertical slice of a product, in which a very limited function set is constructed in full, so as to let early sunlight into places where performance snakes may lurk. What is the difference between the first-milestone-build of the Microsoft process and a rapid prototype? Function. The first-milestone product may not have enough function to be of interest to anyone; the shippable product is defined as such by its completeness in furnishing a useful set of functions, and by its quality, the belief that it works robustly.

Parnas Was Right, and I Was Wrong about Information Hiding

In Chapter 7 I contrast two approaches to the question of how much each team member should be allowed or encouraged to know about each other's designs and code. In the Operating System/360 project, we decided that *all* programmers should see *all* the material—i.e., each programmer having a copy of the project workbook, which came to number over 10,000 pages. Harlan Mills has argued persuasively that "programming should be a public process," that exposing all the work to everybody's gaze helps quality control, both by peer pressure to do things well and by peers actually spotting flaws and bugs.

This view contrasts sharply with David Parnas's teaching that modules of code should be encapsulated with well-defined interfaces, and that the interior of such a module should be the private property of its programmer, not discernible from out-side. Programmers are most effective if shielded from, not ex-posed to, the innards of modules not their own.[13]

I dismissed Parnas's concept as a "recipe for disaster" in Chapter 7. Parnas was right, and I was wrong. I am now con-vinced that information hiding, today often embodied in object-oriented programming, is the only way of raising the level of software design.

One can indeed get disasters with either technique. Mills' technique ensures that programmers can know the detailed se-mantics of the interfaces they work to by knowing what is on the other side. Hiding those semantics leads to system bugs. On the other hand, Parnas's technique is robust under change and is more appropriate in a design-for-change philosophy.

Chapter 16 argues the following:

- Most past progress in software productivity has come from eliminating noninherent difficulties such as awkward ma-chine languages and slow batch turnaround.
- There are not a lot more of these easy pickings.
- Radical progress is going to have to come from attacking the essential difficulties of fashioning complex conceptual con-structs.

The most obvious way to do this recognizes that programs are made up of conceptual chunks much larger than the individ-ual high-level language statement—subroutines, or modules, or classes. If we can limit design and building so that we only do the putting together and parameterization of such chunks from prebuilt collections, we have radically raised the conceptual level, and eliminated the vast amounts of work and the copious opportunities for error that dwell at the individual statement level.

Parnas's information-hiding definition of modules is the first published step in that crucially important research pro-gram, and it is an intellectual ancestor of object-oriented programming. He defined a module as a software entity with its own data model and its own set of operations. Its data can only be accessed via one of its proper operations. The second step was a contribution of several thinkers: the upgrading of the Parnas module into an *abstract data type*, from which many objects could be derived. The abstract data type provides a uniform way of thinking about and specifying module interfaces, and an access discipline that is easy to enforce.

The third step, object-oriented programming, introduces the powerful concept of *inheritance*, whereby classes (data types) take as defaults specified attributes from their ancestors in the class hierarchy.[14] Most of what we hope to gain from object-oriented programming derives in fact from the first step, module encapsulation, plus the idea of prebuilt libraries of modules or classes *that are designed and tested for reuse*. Many people have chosen to ignore the fact that such modules are not just programs, but instead are program products in the sense discussed in Chapter 1. Some people are vainly hoping for significant module reuse without paying the initial cost of building product-quality modules—generalized, robust, tested, and documented. Object-oriented programming and reuse are discussed in Chapters 16 and 17.

How Mythical Is the Man-Month? Boehm's Model and Data

Over the years, there have been many quantitative studies of software productivity and the factors affecting it, especially the trade-offs between project staffing and schedule.

The most substantial study is one done by Barry Boehm of some 63 software projects, mostly aerospace, with about 25 at TRW. His *Software Engineering Economics* contains not only the results but a useful set of cost models of progressive comprehensiveness. Whereas the coefficients in the models are surely different for ordinary commercial software and for aerospace software built to government standards, nevertheless his models are backed by an immense amount of data. I think the book will be a useful classic a generation from now.

His results solidly confirm *The MM-M's* assertion that the trade-off between men and months is far from linear, that the man-month is indeed mythical as a measure of productivity. In particular, he finds:[15]

- There is a cost-optimum schedule time to first shipment, $T = 2.5 (MM)^{1/3}$. That is, the optimum time in months goes as the cube root of the expected effort in man-months, a figure derived from the size estimate and other factors in his model. An optimum staffing curve is a corollary.
- The cost curve rises slowly as the planned schedule gets longer than the optimum. People with more time take more time.
- The cost curve rises sharply as the planned schedule gets shorter than the optimum.
- *Hardly any projects succeed in less than 3/4 of the calculated optimum schedule, regardless of the number of people applied!* This quotable result gives the software manager solid ammunition when higher management is demanding impossible schedule commitments.

How true is Brooks's Law?   There have even been careful studies evaluating the truth of Brooks's (intentionally simplistic) Law, that adding manpower to a late software project makes it later. The best treatment is that of Abdel-Hamid and Madnick, in their ambitious and valuable 1991 book, *Software Project Dynamics: An Integrated Approach.*[16] The book develops a quantitative model of project dynamics. Their chapter on Brooks's Law provides more detailed insight into what happens under various assumptions as to what manpower is added, and when. To investigate this, the authors extend their own careful model of a middle-sized applications project by assuming that new people have a learning curve and accounting for the extra communication and training work. They conclude that "Adding more people to a late project always makes it more costly, but it does not *always* cause it to be completed later [italics theirs]." In particular, adding extra manpower early in the schedule is a much safer maneuver than adding it later, since the new people always have an immediate negative effect, which takes weeks to compensate.

Stutzke develops a simpler model in order to perform a similar investigation, with a similar result.[17] He develops a detailed analysis of the process and costs of assimilating the new workers, including explicitly the diversion of their mentors from the project task itself. He tests his model against an actual project in which manpower was successfully doubled and the original schedule achieved, after a mid-project slip. He treats alternatives to adding more programmers, especially overtime. Most valuable are his many items of practical advice as to how new workers should be added, trained, supported with tools, etc., so as to minimize the disruptive effects of adding them. Especially noteworthy is his comment that new people added late in a development project must be team players willing to pitch in and work within the process, and not attempt to alter or improve the process itself!

Stutzke believes that the added burden of communication in a larger project is a second-order effect and does not model it. It is not clear whether and how Abdel-Hamid and Madnick take it into account. Neither model takes into account the fact that the work must be repartitioned, a process I have often found to be nontrivial.

The "outrageously simplified" statement of Brooks's Law is made more useful by these careful treatments of the proper qualifications. On balance, I stand by the bald statement as the best zeroth-order approximation to the truth, a rule of thumb to warn managers against blindly making the instinctive fix to a late project.

People Are Everything (Well, Almost Everything)

Some readers have found it curious that *The MM-M* devotes most of the essays to the managerial aspects of software engineering, rather than the many technical issues. This bias was due in part to the nature of my role on the IBM Operating System/360 (now MVS/370). More fundamentally, it sprang from a conviction that the quality of the people on a project, and their organization and management, are much more important factors in success than are the tools they use or the technical approaches they take.

Subsequent researches have supported that conviction. Boehm's COCOMO model finds that the quality of the team is by far the largest factor in its success, indeed four times more potent than the next largest factor. Most academic research on software engineering has concentrated on tools. I admire and covet sharp tools. Nevertheless, it is encouraging to see ongoing research efforts on the care, growing, and feeding of people, and on the dynamics of software management.

Peopleware.   A major contribution during recent years has been DeMarco and Lister's 1987 book, *Peopleware: Productive Projects and Teams.* Its underlying thesis is that "The major problems of our work are not so much *technological* as *sociological* in nature." It abounds with gems such as, "The manager's function is not to make people work, it is to make it possible for people to work." It deals with such mundane topics as space, furniture, team meals together. DeMarco and Lister provide real data from their Coding War Games that show stunning correlation between performances of programmers from the same organization, and between workplace characteristics and both productivity and defect levels.

> The top performers' space is quieter, more private, better protected against interruption, and there is more of it. . . . Does it really matter to you . . . whether quiet, space, and privacy help your current people to do better work or [alternatively] help you to attract and keep better people?[18]

I heartily commend the book to all my readers.

Moving projects. DeMarco and Lister give considerable attention to team *fusion*, an intangible but vital property. I think it is management's overlooking fusion that accounts for the readiness I have observed in multilocation companies to move a project from one laboratory to another.

My experience and observation are limited to perhaps a half-dozen moves. I have never seen a successful one. One can move *missions* successfully. But in every case of attempts to move projects, the new team in fact started over, in spite of having good documentation, some well-advanced designs, and some of the people from the sending team. I think it is the breaking of fusion of the old team that aborts the embryonic product, and brings about restart.

The Power of Giving Up Power

If one believes, as I have argued at many places in this book, that creativity comes from individuals and not from structures or processes, then a central question facing the software manager is how to design structure and process so as to enhance, rather than inhibit, creativity and initiative. Fortunately, this problem is not peculiar to software organizations, and great thinkers have worked on it. E. F. Schumacher, in his classic, *Small is Beautiful: Economics as if People Mattered*, proposes a theory of organizing enterprises to maximize the creativity and joy of the workers. For his first principle he chooses the "Principle of Subsidiary Function" from the Encyclical *Quadragesimo Anno* of Pope Pius XI:

> *It is an injustice and at the same time a grave evil and disturbance of right order to assign to a greater and higher association what lesser and subordinate organizations can do. For every social activity ought of its very nature to furnish help to the members of the body social and never destroy and absorb them. . . . Those in command should be sure that the more perfectly a graduated order is*

preserved among the various associations, in observing the princi-ple of subsidiary function, the stronger will be the social authority and effectiveness and the happier and more prosperous the condition of the State.[19]

Schumacher goes on to interpret:

The Principle of Subsidiary Function teaches us that the centre will gain in authority and effectiveness if the freedom and responsibility of the lower formations are carefully preserved, with the result that the organization as a whole will be "happier and more prosperous."

How can such a structure be achieved?. . . . The large orga-nization will consist of many semi-autonomous units, which we may call quasi-firms. *Each of them will have a large amount of freedom, to give the greatest possible chance to creativity and en-trepreneurship. . . . Each quasi-firm must have both a profit and loss account, and a balance sheet.*[20]

Among the most exciting developments in software engi-neering are the early stages of putting such organizational ideas into practice. First, the microcomputer revolution created a new software industry of hundreds of start-up firms, all of them starting small, and marked by enthusiasm, freedom, and crea-tivity. The industry is changing now, as many small companies are being acquired by larger ones. It remains to be seen if the larger acquirers will understand the importance of preserving the creativity of smallness.

More remarkably, high management in some large firms have undertaken to delegate power down to individual software project teams, making them approach Schumacher's quasi-firms in structure and responsibility. They are surprised and de-lighted at the results.

Jim McCarthy of Microsoft described to me his experience at emancipating his teams:

Each feature team (30–40 people) owns its feature set, its schedule, and even its process of how to define, build, ship. The team is made up for four or five specialties, including building, testing, and writing. The team settles squabbles; the bosses don't. I can't emphasize enough the importance of empowerment, of the team being accountable to itself for its success.

Earl Wheeler, retired head of IBM's software business, told me his experience in undertaking the downward delegation of power long centralized in IBM's division managements:

The key thrust [of recent years] was delegating power down. It was like magic! Improved quality, productivity, morale. We have small teams, with no central control. The teams own the process, but they have to have one. They have many different processes. They own the schedule, but they feel the pressure of the market. This pressure causes them to reach for tools on their own.

Conversations with individual team members, of course, show both an appreciation of the power and freedom that is delegated, and a somewhat more conservative estimate of how much control really is relinquished. Nevertheless, the delegation achieved is clearly a step in the right direction. It yields exactly the benefits Pius XI predicted: the center gains in real authority by delegating power, and the organization as a whole is happier and more prosperous.

What's the Biggest New Surprise? Millions of Computers

Every software guru I have talked with admits to being caught by surprise by the microcomputer revolution and its outgrowth, the shrink-wrapped software industry. This is beyond doubt the crucial change of the two decades since *The MM-M*. It has many implications for software engineering.

The microcomputer revolution has changed how everybody uses computers.   Schumacher stated the challenge more than 20 years ago:

What is it that we really require from the scientists and technolo-

gists? I should answer: We need methods and equipment which are
- *cheap enough so that they are accessible to virtually everyone;*
- *suitable for small-scale application; and*
- *compatible with man's need for creativity.*[21]

These are exactly the wonderful properties that the microcomputer revolution has brought to the computer industry and to its users, now the general public. The average American can now afford not only a computer of his own, but a suite of software that 20 years ago would have cost a king's salary. Each of Schumacher's goals is worth contemplating; the degree to which each has been achieved is worth savoring, especially the last. In area after area, new means of self-expression are accessible to ordinary people as well as to professionals.

Partly the enhancement comes in other fields as it has in software creation—in the removal of accidental difficulties. Written manuscripts used to be accidentally rigidified by the time and cost of retyping to incorporate changes. On a 300-page work, one might go through retyping every three to six months, but in between, one just kept marking the manuscript. One could not easily assess what the changes had done to the flow of the logic and the rhythm of the words. Now, manuscripts have become wondrously fluid.[22]

The computer has brought a similar fluidity to many other media: artistic drawings, building plans, mechanical drawings, musical compositions, photographs, video sequences, slide presentations, multimedia works, and even to spreadsheets. In each case, the manual method of production required recopying the bulky unchanged parts in order to see changes in context. Now we enjoy for each medium the same benefits that time-sharing brought to software creation—the ability to revise and to assess instantly the effect without losing one's train of thought.

Creativity is also enhanced by new and flexible auxiliary tools. For prose production, as one example, we are now served by spelling checkers, grammar checkers, style advisors, bibliographic systems, and the remarkable ability to see pages concurrently formatted into final layout. We do not yet appreciate what instantaneous encyclopedias or the infinite resources of the World-Wide Web will mean for a writer's impromptu research.

Most important, the new fluidity of the media makes easy the exploration of many radically different alternatives when a creative work is just taking form. Here is another case where an order of magnitude in a quantitative parameter, here change-time, makes a qualitative difference in how one goes about a task.

Tools for drawing enable building designers to explore many more options per hour of creative investment. The connection of computers to synthesizers, with software for automatically generating or playing scores, makes it much easier to capture keyboard doodles. Digital photograph manipulation, as with Adobe Photoshop, enables minutes-long experiments that would take hours in a darkroom. Spreadsheets enable the easy exploration of dozens of "what if" alternative scenarios.

Finally, wholly new creative media have been enabled by the ubiquity of the personal computer. Hypertexts, proposed by Vannevar Bush in 1945, are practical only with computers.[23] Multimedia presentations and experiences were big deals—just too much trouble—before the personal computer and the rich, cheap software available for it. Virtual-environment systems, not yet cheap or ubiquitous, will become so, and will be yet another creative medium.

The microcomputer revolution has changed how everybody builds software. The software processes of the 1970s have themselves been altered by the microprocessor revolution and the technology advances that enabled it. Many of the accidental difficulties of those software building processes have been eliminated. Fast individual computers are now the routine tools of the software developer, so that turnaround time is an almost obsolete concept. The personal computer of today is not only faster than the supercomputer of 1960, it is faster than the Unix work-station of 1985. All of this means that compilation is fast even on the humblest machines, and large memories have eliminated waits for disk-based linking. Large memories also make it reasonable to keep symbol tables in memory with object code, so high-level debugging without recompilation is routine.

In the last 20 years, we have come almost completely through the use of time-sharing as the methodology for constructing software. In 1975, time-sharing had just replaced batch computing as the most common technique. The network was used to give the software builder access both to shared files and to a shared powerful engine for compilation, linking, and testing. Today, the personal workstation provides the computing engine, and the network primarily gives shared access to the files that are the team's developing work-product. Client-server systems make shared access to check-in, build, and the application of test cases a different and simpler process.

Similar advances in user interfaces have occurred. The WIMP interface provides much more convenient editing of program texts as well as of English-language texts. The 24-line, 72-column screen has been replaced by full-page or even two-page screens, so programmers can see much more context for changes they are making.

Whole New Software Industry—Shrink-Wrapped Software

Alongside the classical software industry there has exploded another. Product unit sales run in hundreds of thousands, even millions. Entire rich software packages can be had for less than the cost of one supported programmer-day. The two industries are different in many ways, and they coexist.

The classical software industry.   In 1975, the software industry had several identifiable and somewhat different components, all of which still exist today:

- Computer vendors, who provide operating systems, compilers, and utilities for their products.

- Application users, such as the MIS shops of utilities, banks, insurance companies, and government agencies, who build application packages for their own use.
- Custom application builders, who contract to build proprietary packages for users. Many of these contractors specialize in defense applications, where requirements, standards, and marketing procedures are peculiar.
- Commercial package developers, who at that time developed mostly large applications for specialized markets, such as statistical analysis packages and CAD systems.

Tom DeMarco notes the fragmentation of the classical software industry, especially the application-user component:

> *What I didn't expect: the field has partitioned into niches. How you do something is much more a function of the niche than it is the use of general systems analysis methods, general languages, and general testing techniques. Ada was the last of the general-purpose languages, and it has become a niche language.*

In the routine commercial application niche, fourth-generation languages have made powerful contributions. Boehm says, "Most successful 4GLs are the result of someone's codifying a piece of an application domain in terms of options and parameters." The most pervasive of these 4GLs are application generators and combined database-communications packages with inquiry languages.

Operating system worlds have coalesced.   In 1975, operating systems abounded: each hardware vendor had at least one proprietary operating system per product line; many had two. How different things are today! Open systems are the watchword, and there are only five significant operating systems environments into which people market applications packages (in chronological order):

- The IBM MVS and VM environments
- The DEC VMS environment
- The Unix environment, in one flavor or another
- The IBM PC environment, whether DOS, OS-2, or Windows
- The Apple Macintosh environment.

The shrink-wrapped industry.   For the developer in the shrink-wrapped industry, the economics are entirely different from those of the classical industry: development cost is divided by large quantities; packaging and marketing costs loom large. In the classical in-house application development industry, schedule and the details of function were negotiable, development cost might not be; in the fiercely competitive open market, schedule and function quite dominate development cost.

As one would expect, the starkly different economics have given rise to rather different programming cultures. The classical industry tended to be dominated by large firms with established management styles and work cultures. The shrink-wrapped industry, on the other hand, began as hundreds of start-ups, freewheeling and fiercely focused on getting the job done rather than on process. In this climate, there has always been a much greater recognition of the talent of the individual programmer, an implicit awareness that great designs come from great designers. The start-up culture has the capability of rewarding star performers in proportion to their contributions; in the classical software industry the sociology of corporations and their salary-management plans have always made this difficult. It is not surprising that many of the stars of the new generation have gravitated to the shrink-wrapped industry.

Buy *and* Build—Shrink-Wrapped Packages As Components

Radically better software robustness and productivity are to be had only by moving up a level, and making programs by the composition of modules, or objects. An especially promising trend is the use of mass-market packages as the platforms on which richer and more customized products are built. A truck-tracking system is built on a shrink-wrapped database and communications package; so is a student information system. The want ads in computer magazines offer hundreds of Hypercard stacks and customized templates for Excel, dozens of special functions in Pascal for MiniCad or functions in AutoLisp for AutoCad.

Metaprogramming. Building Hypercard stacks, Excel templates, or MiniCad functions is sometimes called *metaprogramming*, the construction of a new layer that customizes function for a subset of a package's users. The metaprogramming concept is not new, only resurgent and renamed. In the early 1960s, computer vendors and many big management information systems (MIS) shops had small groups of specialists who crafted whole application programming languages out of macros in assembly language. Eastman Kodak's MIS shop had a house application language defined on the IBM 7080 macroassembler. Similarly with IBM's OS/360 Queued Telecommunications Access Method, one could read many pages of an ostensibly assembly-language telecommunications program before encountering a machine-level instruction. Now the chunks offered by the metaprogrammer are many times larger than those macros. This development of secondary markets is most encouraging—while we have been waiting to see an effective market in C + + classes develop, a market in reusable metaprograms has grown up unremarked.

This really does attack essence. Because the build-on-package phenomenon does not today affect the average MIS programmer, it is not yet very visible to the software engineering discipline. Nevertheless, it will grow rapidly, because it does attack the essence of fashioning conceptual constructs. The shrink-wrapped package provides a big module of function, with an elaborate but proper interface, and its internal conceptual structure does not have to be designed at all. High-function software products such as Excel or 4th Dimension are big modules indeed, but they serve as known, documented, tested modules with which to build customized systems. Next-level application builders get richness of function, a shorter development time, a tested component, better documentation, and radically lower cost.

The difficulty, of course, is that the shrink-wrapped software package is designed as a stand-alone entity whose functions and interfaces metaprogrammers cannot change. Moreover, and more seriously, shrink-wrapped package builders seemingly have little incentive to make their products suitable as modules in a larger system. I think that perception is wrong, that there is an untapped market in providing packages designed to facilitate metaprogrammer use.

So what is needed?   We can identify four levels of users of shrink-wrapped packages:

- The as-is user, who operates the application in straightforward manner, content with the functions and the interface the designers provided.
- The metaprogrammer, who builds templates or functions on top of a single application, using the interface provided, principally to save work for the end user.
- The external function writer, who hand-codes added functions into an application. These are essentially new application language primitives that call out to separate code modules written in a general-purpose language. One needs the capability to interface these new functions to the application as intercepted commands, as callbacks, or as overloaded functions.
- The metaprogrammer who uses one, or especially several, applications as components in a larger system. This is the user whose needs are poorly met today. This is also the use

which promises substantial effectiveness gains in building new applications.

For this last user, a shrink-wrapped application needs an additional documented interface, the metaprogramming interface (MPI). It needs several capabilities. First, the metaprogram needs to be in control of an ensemble of applications, whereas normally each application assumes it is itself in control. The ensemble must control the user interface, which ordinarily the application assumes it is doing. The ensemble must be able to invoke any application function as if its command string had come from the user. It should receive output from the application as if it is the screen, except that it needs the output parsed into logical units of suitable datatypes, rather than the text string that would have been displayed. Some applications, such as FoxPro, have wormholes that allow one to pass a command string in, but the information one gets back is skimpy and unparsed. The wormhole is an *ad hoc* fix for a need that demands a general, designed solution.

It is powerful to have a scripting language for controlling the interactions among the ensemble of applications. Unix first provided this kind of function, with its pipes and its standard ASCII-string file format. Today AppleScript is a rather good example.

The State and Future of Software Engineering

I once asked Jim Ferrell, chairman of the Department of Chemical Engineering at North Carolina State University, to relate the history of chemical engineering, as distinguished from chemistry. He thereupon gave a wonderful impromptu hour-long account, beginning with the existence from antiquity of many different production processes for many products, from steel to bread to perfume. He told how Professor Arthur D. Little founded a Department of Industrial Chemistry at MIT in 1918, to find, develop, and teach a common base of technique shared by all the processes. First came rules of thumb, then empirical nomograms, then formulas for designing particular components, then mathematical models for heat transport, mass transport, momentum transport in single vessels.

As Ferrell's tale unfolded, I was struck by the many parallels between the development of chemical engineering and that of software engineering, almost exactly fifty years later. Parnas reproves me for writing about *software engineering* at all. He contrasts the software discipline with electrical engineering and feels it is a presumption to call what we do engineering. He may be right that the field will never develop into an engineering discipline with as precise and all-encompassing a mathematical base as electrical engineering has. After all, software engineering, like chemical engineering, is concerned with the nonlinear problems of scaling up into industrial-scale processes, and like industrial engineering, it is permanently confounded by the complexities of human behavior.

Nevertheless, the course and timing of chemical engineering's development leads me to believe that software engineering at age 27 may be not hopeless but merely immature, as chemical engineering was in 1945. It was only after WWII that chemical engineers really addressed the behavior of closed-loop interconnected continuous-flow systems.

The distinctive concerns of software engineering are today exactly those set forth in Chapter 1:

- How to design and build a set of programs into a *system*
- How to design and build a program or a system into a robust, tested, documented, supported *product*
- How to maintain intellectual control over *complexity* in large doses.

The tar pit of software engineering will continue to be sticky for a long time to come. One can expect the human race to continue attempting systems just within or just beyond our reach; and software systems are perhaps the most intricate of man's handiworks. This complex craft will demand our continual development of the discipline, our learning to compose in larger units, our best use of new tools, our best adaptation of proven engineering management methods, liberal application of common sense, and a God-given humility to recognize our fallibility and limitations.

Epilogue
Fifty Years of Wonder, Excitement, and Joy

Still vivid in my mind is the wonder and delight with which I—then 13 years old—read the account of the August 7, 1944, dedication of the Harvard Mark I computer, an electromechanical marvel for which Howard Aiken was the architect and IBM engineers Clair Lake, Benjamin Durfee, and Francis Hamilton were the implementation designers. Equally wonder-provoking was the reading of Vannevar Bush's "That We May Think" paper in the April 1945 *Atlantic Monthly,* in which he proposed organizing knowledge as a big hypertext web and giving users machines for both following existing trails and blazing new trails of associations.

My passion for computers got another strong boost in 1952, when a summer job at IBM in Endicott, New York, gave me hands-on experience in programming the IBM 604 and formal instruction in programming IBM's 701, its first stored-program machine. Graduate school under Aiken and Iverson at Harvard made my career dream a reality, and I was hooked for life. To only a fraction of the human race does God give the privilege of earning one's bread doing what one would have gladly pursued free, for passion. I am very thankful.

It is hard to imagine a more exciting time to have lived as a computer devotee. From mechanisms to vacuum tubes to transistors to integrated circuits, the technology has exploded. The first computer on which I worked, fresh out of Harvard, was the

IBM 7030 Stretch supercomputer. Stretch reigned as the world's fastest computer from 1961 to 1964; nine copies were delivered. My Macintosh Powerbook is today not only faster, with a larger memory and bigger disk, it is a thousand times cheaper. (*Five* thousand times cheaper in constant dollars.) We have seen in turn the computer revolution, the electronic computer revolution, the minicomputer revolution, and the microcomputer revolution, each bringing orders-of-magnitude more computers.

The computer-related intellectual discipline has exploded as has the technology. When I was a graduate student in the mid-1950s, I could read *all* the journals and conference proceedings; I could stay current in *all* the discipline. Today my intellectual life has seen me regretfully kissing subdiscipline interests goodbye one by one, as my portfolio has continuously overflowed beyond mastery. Too many interests, too many exciting opportunities for learning, research, and thought. What a marvelous predicament! Not only is the end not in sight, the pace is not slackening. We have many future joys.

Notes and References

Chapter 1

1. Ershov considers this not only a woe, but also a part of the joy. A. P. Ershov, "Aesthetics and the human factor in programming," *CACM*, **15**, 7 (July, 1972), pp. 501–505.

Chapter 2

1. V. A. Vyssotsky of Bell Telephone Laboratories estimates that a large project can sustain a manpower buildup of 30 percent per year. More than that strains and even inhibits the evolution of the essential informal structure and its communication pathways discussed in Chapter 7.
   F. J. Corbató of MIT points out that a long project must anticipate a turnover of 20 percent per year, and these must be both technically trained and integrated into the formal structure.

2. C. Portman of International Computers Limited says, *"When everything has been seen to work, all integrated, you have four more months work to do."* Several other sets of schedule divisions are given in Wolverton, R. W., "The cost of developing large-scale software," *IEEE Trans. on Computers*, **C-23,** 6 (June, 1974) pp. 615–636.

3. Figures 2.5 through 2.8 are due to Jerry Ogdin, who in quoting my example from an earlier publication of this chapter much improved its illustration. Ogdin, J. L., "The Mongolian hordes versus superprogrammer," *Infosystems* (Dec., 1972), pp. 20–23.

Chapter 3

1. Sackman, H., W. J. Erikson, and E. E. Grant, "Exploratory experimental studies comparing online and offline programming performance," *CACM*, **11**, 1 (Jan., 1968), pp. 3–11.

2. Mills, H., "Chief programmer teams, principles, and procedures," IBM Federal Systems Division Report FSC 71–5108, Gaithersburg, Md., 1971.

3. Baker, F. T., "Chief programmer team management of production programming," *IBM Sys. J.*, **11**, 1 (1972).

Chapter 4

1. Eschapasse, M., *Reims Cathedral*, Caisse Nationale des Monuments Historiques, Paris, 1967.

2. Brooks, F. P., "Architectural philosophy," in W. Buchholz (ed.), *Planning A Computer System*. New York: McGraw-Hill, 1962.

3. Blaauw, G. A., "Hardware requirements for the fourth generation," in F. Gruenberger (ed.), *Fourth Generation Computers*. Englewood Cliffs, N.J.: Prentice-Hall, 1970.

4. Brooks, F. P., and K. E. Iverson, *Automatic Data Processing, System/360 Edition*. New York: Wiley, 1969, Chapter 5.

5. Glegg, G. L., *The Design of Design*. Cambridge: Cambridge Univ. Press, 1969, says *"At first sight, the idea of any rules or principles being superimposed on the creative mind seems more likely to hinder than to help, but this is quite untrue in practice. Disciplined thinking focusses inspiration rather than blinkers it."*

6. Conway, R. W., "The PL/C Compiler," *Proceedings of a Conf. on Definition and Implementation of Universal Programming Languages*. Stuttgart, 1970.

7. For a good discussion of the necessity for programming technology, see C. H. Reynolds, "What's wrong with com-

puter programming management?" in G. F. Weinwuim (ed.), *On the Management of Computer Programming*. Philadelphia: Auerbach, 1971, pp. 35–42.

Chapter 5

1. Strachey, C., "Review of *Planning a Computer System*," *Comp. J.*, **5**, 2 (July, 1962), pp. 152–153.

2. This applies only to the control programs. Some of the compiler teams in the OS/360 effort were building their third or fourth systems, and the excellence of their products shows it.

3. Shell, D. L., "The Share 709 system: a cooperative effort"; Greenwald, I. D., and M. Kane, "The Share 709 system: programming and modification"; Boehm, E. M., and T. B. Steel, Jr., "The Share 709 system: machine implementation of symbolic programming"; all in *JACM*, **6**, 2 (April, 1959), pp. 123–140.

Chapter 6

1. Neustadt, R. E., *Presidential Power*. New York: Wiley, 1960, Chapter 2.

2. Backus, J. W., "The syntax and semantics of the proposed international algebraic language." *Proc. Intl. Conf. Inf. Proc. UNESCO*, Paris, 1959, published by R. Oldenbourg, Munich, and Butterworth, London. Besides this, a whole collection of papers on the subject is contained in T. B. Steel, Jr. (ed.), *Formal Language Description Languages for Computer Programming*. Amsterdam: North Holland, (1966).

3. Lucas, P., and K. Walk, "On the formal description of PL/I," *Annual Review in Automatic Programming Language*. New York: Wiley, 1962, Chapter 2, p. 2.

4. Iverson, K. E., *A Programming Language*. New York: Wiley, 1962, Chapter 2.

5. Falkoff, A. D., K. E. Iverson, E. H. Sussenguth, "A formal description of System/360," *IBM Systems Journal*, **3**, 3 (1964), pp. 198–261.

6. Bell, C. G., and A. Newell, *Computer Structures*. New York: McGraw-Hill, 1970, pp. 120–136, 517–541.

7. Bell, C. G., private communication.

Chapter 7

1. Parnas, D. L., "Information distribution aspects of design methodology," Carnegie-Mellon Univ., Dept. of Computer Science Technical Report, February, 1971.

2. Copyright 1939, 1940 Street & Smith Publications, Copyright 1950, 1967 by Robert A. Heinlein. Published by arrangement with Spectrum Literary Agency.

Chapter 8

1. Sackman, H., W. J. Erikson, and E. E. Grant, "Exploratory experimentation studies comparing online and offline programming performance," *CACM*, **11**, 1 (Jan., 1968), pp. 3–11.

2. Nanus, B., and L. Farr, "Some cost contributors to large-scale programs," *AFIPS Proc. SJCC*, **25** (Spring, 1964), pp. 239–248.

3. Weinwurm, G. F., "Research in the management of computer programming," Report SP-2059, System Development Corp., Santa Monica, 1965.

4. Morin, L. H., "Estimation of resources for computer programming projects," M. S. thesis, Univ. of North Carolina, Chapel Hill, 1974.

5. Portman, C., private communication.

6. An unpublished 1964 study by E. F. Bardain shows programmers realizing 27 percent productive time. (Quoted by

D. B. Mayer and A. W. Stalnaker, "Selection and evaluation of computer personnel," *Proc. 23rd ACM Conf.*, 1968, p. 661.)

7. Aron, J., private communication.

8. Paper given at a panel session and not included in the *AFIPS Proceedings*.

9. Wolverton, R. W., "The cost of developing large-scale software," *IEEE Trans. on Computers*, **C-23**, 6 (June, 1974) pp. 615–636. This important recent paper contains data on many of the issues of this chapter, as well as confirming the productivity conclusions.

10. Corbató, F. J., "Sensitive issues in the design of multi-use systems," lecture at the opening of the Honeywell EDP Technology Center, 1968.

11. W. M. Taliaffero also reports a constant productivity of 2400 statements/year in assembler, Fortran, and Cobol. See "Modularity. The key to system growth potential," *Software*, **1**, 3 (July 1971) pp. 245–257.

12. E. A. Nelson's System Development Corp. Report TM-3225, *Management Handbook for the Estimation of Computer Programming Costs*, shows a 3-to-1 productivity improvement for high-level language (pp. 66–67), although his standard deviations are wide.

Chapter 9

1. Brooks, F. P. and K. E. Iverson, *Automatic Data Processing, System/360 Edition*. New York: Wiley, 1969, Chapter 6.

2. Knuth, D. E., *The Art of Computer Programming*, Vols. 1–3. Reading, Mass.: Addison-Wesley, 1968, ff.

Chapter 10

1. Conway, M. E., "How do committees invent?" *Datamation*, **14**, 4 (April, 1968), pp. 28–31.

Chapter 11

1. Speech at Oglethorpe University, May 22, 1932.

2. An illuminating account of Multics experience on two successive systems is in F. J. Corbató, J. H. Saltzer, and C. T. Clingen, "Multics—the first seven years," *AFIPS Proc SJCC*, **40** (1972), pp. 571–583.

3. Cosgrove, J., "Needed: a new planning framework," *Datamation*, **17**, 23 (Dec., 1971), pp. 37–39.

4. The matter of design change is complex, and I oversimplify here. See J. H. Saltzer, "Evolutionary design of complex systems," in D. Eckman (ed.), *Systems: Research and Design.* New York: Wiley, 1961. When all is said and done, however, I still advocate building a pilot system whose discarding is planned.

5. Campbell, E., "Report to the AEC Computer Information Meeting," December, 1970. The phenomenon is also discussed by J. L. Ogdin in "Designing reliable software," *Datamation*, **18**, 7 (July, 1972), pp. 71–78. My experienced friends seem divided rather evenly as to whether the curve finally goes down again.

6. Lehman, M., and L. Belady, "Programming system dynamics," given at the ACM SIGOPS Third Symposium on Operating System Principles, October, 1971.

7. Lewis, C. S., *Mere Christianity.* New York: Macmillan, 1960, p. 54.

Chapter 12

1. See also J. W. Pomeroy, "A guide to programming tools and techniques," *IBM Sys. J.*, **11**, 3 (1972), pp. 234–254.

2. Landy, B., and R. M. Needham, "Software engineering techniques used in the development of the Cambridge Multiple-Access System," *Software*, **1**, 2 (April, 1971), pp. 167–173.

3. Corbató, F. J., "PL/I as a tool for system programming," *Datamation*, **15,** 5 (May, 1969), pp. 68–76.

4. Hopkins, M., "Problems of PL/I for system programming," IBM Research Report RC 3489, Yorktown Heights, N.Y., August 5, 1971.

5. Corbató, F. J., J. H. Saltzer, and C. T. Clingen, "Multics— the first seven years," *AFIPS Proc SJCC,* **40** (1972), pp. 571– 582. *"Only a half-dozen areas which were written in PL/I have been recoded in machine language for reasons of squeezing out the utmost in performance. Several programs, originally in machine language, have been recoded in PL/I to increase their maintainability."*

6. To quote Corbató's paper cited in reference 3: *"PL/I is here now and the alternatives are still untested."* But see a quite contrary view, well-documented, in Henricksen, J. O. and R. E. Merwin, "Programming language efficiency in real-time software systems," *AFIPS Proc SJCC,* **40** (1972) pp. 155–161.

7. Not all agree. Harlan Mills says, in a private communication, *"My experience begins to tell me that in production programming the person to put at the terminal is the secretary. The idea is to make programming a more public practice, under common scrutiny of many team members, rather than a private art."*

8. Harr, J., "Programming Experience for the Number 1 Electronic Switching System," paper given at the 1969 SJCC.

Chapter 13

1. Vyssotsky, V. A., "Common sense in designing testable software," lecture at The Computer Program Test Methods Symposium, Chapel Hill, N.C., 1972. Most of Vyssotsky's lecture is contained in Hetzel, W. C. (ed.), *Program Test Methods.* Englewood Cliffs, N.J.: Prentice-Hall, 1972, pp. 41– 47.

2. Wirth, N., "Program development by stepwise refinement," *CACM* **14,** 4 (April, 1971), pp. 221–227. See also

Mills, H. "Top-down programming in large systems," in R. Rustin (ed.). *Debugging Techniques in Large Systems*. Englewood Cliffs, N.J.: Prentice-Hall, 1971, pp. 41–55 and Baker, F. T., "System quality through structured programming," *AFIPS Proc FJCC*, **41-I** (1972), pp. 339–343.

3. Dahl, O. J., E. W. Dijkstra, and C. A. R. Hoare, *Structured Programming*. London and New York: Academic Press, 1972. This volume contains the fullest treatment. See also Dijkstra's germinal letter, "GOTO statement considered harmful," *CACM*, **11,** 3 (March, 1968), pp. 147–148.

4. Böhm, C., and A. Jacopini, "Flow diagrams, Turing machines, and languages with only two formation rules," *CACM*, **9,** 5 (May, 1966), pp. 366–371.

5. Codd, E. F., E. S. Lowry, E. McDonough, and C. A. Scalzi, "Multiprogramming STRETCH: Feasibility considerations," *CACM*, **2,** 11 (Nov., 1959), pp. 13–17.

6. Strachey, C., "Time sharing in large fast computers," *Proc. Int. Conf. on Info. Processing*, UNESCO (June, 1959), pp. 336–341. See also Codd's remarks on p. 341, where he reported progress on work like that proposed in Strachey's paper.

7. Corbató, F. J., M. Merwin-Daggett, R. C. Daley, "An experimental time-sharing system," *AFIPS Proc. SJCC*, **2,** (1962), pp. 335–344. Reprinted in S. Rosen, *Programming Systems and Languages*. New York: McGraw-Hill, 1967, pp. 683–698.

8. Gold, M. M., "A methodology for evaluating time-shared computer system usage," Ph.D. dissertation, Carnegie-Mellon University, 1967, p. 100.

9. Gruenberger, F., "Program testing and validating," *Datamation*, **14,** 7, (July, 1968), pp. 39–47.

10. Ralston, A., *Introduction to Programming and Computer Science*. New York: McGraw-Hill, 1971, pp. 237–244.

11. Brooks, F. P., and K. E. Iverson, *Automatic Data Processing, System/360 Edition*. New York: Wiley, 1969, pp. 296–299.

12. A good treatment of development of specifications and of system build and test is given by F. M. Trapnell, "A systematic approach to the development of system programs," *AFIPS Proc SJCC*, **34** (1969) pp. 411–418.

13. A real-time system will require an environment simulator. See, for example, M. G. Ginzberg, "Notes on testing real-time system programs," *IBM Sys. J.*, **4**, 1 (1965), pp. 58–72.

14. Lehman, M., and L. Belady, "Programming system dynamics," given at the ACM SIGOPS Third Symposium on Operating System Principles, October, 1971.

Chapter 14

1. See C. H. Reynolds, "What's wrong with computer programming management?" in G. F. Weinwurm (ed.), *On the Management of Computer Programming*. Philadelphia: Auerbach, 1971, pp. 35–42.

2. King, W. R., and T. A. Wilson, "Subjective time estimates in critical path planning—a preliminary analysis," *Mgt. Sci.*, **13**, 5 (Jan., 1967), pp. 307–320, and sequel, W. R. King, D. M. Witterrongel, K. D. Hezel, "On the analysis of critical path time estimating behavior," *Mgt. Sci.*, **14**, 1 (Sept., 1967), pp. 79–84.

3. For a fuller discussion, see Brooks, F. P., and K. E. Iverson, *Automatic Data Processing, System/360 Edition*, New York: Wiley, 1969, pp. 428–430.

4. Private communication.

Chapter 15

1. Goldstine, H. H., and J. von Neumann, "Planning and coding problems for an electronic computing instrument," Part II, Vol. 1, report prepared for the U.S. Army Ordinance Department, 1947; reprinted in J. von Neumann, *Collected Works*, A. H. Taub (ed.), Vol. v., New York: McMillan, pp. 80–151.

2. Private communication, 1957. The argument is published in Iverson, K. E., "The Use of APL in Teaching," Yorktown, N.Y.: IBM Corp., 1969.

3. Another list of techniques for PL/I is given by A. B. Walter and M. Bohl in "From better to best—tips for good programming," *Software Age*, **3**, 11 (Nov., 1969), pp. 46–50.

   The same techniques can be used in Algol and even Fortran. D. E. Lang of the University of Colorado has a Fortran formatting program called STYLE that accomplishes such a result. See also D. D. McCracken and G. M. Weinberg, "How to write a readable FORTRAN program," *Datamation*, **18**, 10 (Oct., 1972), pp. 73–77.

Chapter 16

1. The essay entitled "No Silver Bullet" is from Information Processing 1986, the Proceedings of the IFIP Tenth World Computing Conference, edited by H.-J. Kugler (1986), pp. 1069–76. Reprinted with the kind permission of IFIP and Elsevier Science B. V., Amsterdam, The Netherlands.

2. Parnas, D. L., "Designing software for ease of extension and contraction," *IEEE Trans. on SE*, **5**, 2 (March, 1979), pp. 128–138.

3. Booch, G., "Object-oriented design," in *Software Engineering with Ada*. Menlo Park, Calif.: Benjamin/Cummings, 1983.

4. Mostow, J., ed., Special Issue on Artificial Intelligence and Software Engineering, *IEEE Trans. on SE*, **11**, 11 (Nov., 1985).

5. Parnas, D. L., "Software aspects of strategic defense systems," *Communications of the ACM*, **28**, 12 (Dec., 1985), pp. 1326–1335. Also in *American Scientist*, **73**, 5 (Sept.-Oct., 1985), pp. 432–440.

6. Balzer, R., "A 15-year perspective on automatic programming," in Mostow, *op. cit.*

7. Mostow, op. cit.

8. Parnas, 1985, op. cit.

9. Raeder, G., "A survey of current graphical programming techniques," in R. B. Grafton and T. Ichikawa, eds., Special Issue on Visual Programming, *Computer,* **18,** 8 (Aug., 1985), pp. 11–25.

10. The topic is discussed in Chapter 15 of this book.

11. Mills, H. D., "Top-down programming in large systems," *Debugging Techniques in Large Systems,* R. Rustin, ed., Englewood Cliffs, N.J., Prentice-Hall, 1971.

12. Boehm, B. W., "A spiral model of software development and enhancement," *Computer,* **20,** 5 (May, 1985), pp. 43–57.

Chapter 17

Material quoted without citation is from personal communications.

1. Brooks, F. P., "No silver bullet—essence and accidents of software engineering," in *Information Processing 86,* H. J. Kugler, ed. Amsterdam: Elsevier Science (North Holland), 1986, pp. 1069–1076.

2. Brooks, F. P., "No silver bullet—essence and accidents of software engineering," *Computer* **20,** 4 (April, 1987), pp. 10–19.

3. Several of the letters, and a reply, appeared in the July, 1987 issue of *Computer.*

   It is a special pleasure to observe that whereas "NSB" received no awards, Bruce M. Skwiersky's review of it was selected as the best review published in *Computing Reviews* in 1988. E. A. Weiss, "Editorial," *Computing Reviews* (June, 1989), pp. 283–284, both announces the award and reprints Skwiersky's review. The review has one significant error: "sixfold" should be "10^6."

4. "According to Aristotle, and in Scholastic philosophy, an accident is a quality which does not belong to a thing by right of that thing's essential or substantial nature but occurs in it as an effect of other causes." *Webster's New International Dictionary of the English Language,* 2d ed., Springfield, Mass.: G. C. Merriam, 1960.

5. Sayers, Dorothy L., *The Mind of the Maker.* New York: Harcourt, Brace, 1941.

6. Glass, R. L., and S. A. Conger, "Research software tasks: Intellectual or clerical?" *Information and Management,* **23,** 4 (1992). The authors report a measurement of software requirements specification to be about 80% intellectual and 20% clerical. Fjelstadt and Hamlen, 1979, get essentially the same results for application software maintenance. I know of no attempt to measure this fraction for the whole end-to-end task.

7. Herzberg, F., B. Mausner, and B. B. Sayderman. *The Motivation to Work,* 2nd ed. London: Wiley, 1959.

8. Cox, B. J., "There is a silver bullet," *Byte* (Oct., 1990), pp. 209–218.

9. Harel, D., "Biting the silver bullet: Toward a brighter future for system development," *Computer* (Jan., 1992), pp. 8–20.

10. Parnas, D. L., "Software aspects of strategic defense systems," *Communications of the ACM,* **28,** 12 (Dec., 1985), pp. 1326–1335.

11. Turski, W. M., "And no philosophers' stone, either," in *Information Processing 86,* H. J. Kugler, ed. Amsterdam: Elsevier Science (North Holland), 1986, pp. 1077–1080.

12. Glass, R. L., and S. A. Conger, "Research Software Tasks: Intellectual or Clerical?" *Information and Management,* **23,** 4 (1992), pp. 183–192.

13. *Review of Electronic Digital Computers, Proceedings of a Joint AIEE-IRE Computer Conference* (Philadelphia, Dec. 10–12, 1951). New York: American Institute of Electrical Engineers, pp. 13–20.

14. *Ibid.,* pp. 36, 68, 71, 97.

15. *Proceedings of the Eastern Joint Computer Conference,* (Washington, Dec. 8–10, 1953). New York: Institute of Electrical Engineers, pp. 45–47.

16. *Proceedings of the 1955 Western Joint Computer Conference* (Los

Angeles, March 1–3, 1955). New York: Institute of Electrical Engineers.

17. Everett, R. R., C. A. Zraket, and H. D. Bennington, "SAGE—A data processing system for air defense," *Proceedings of the Eastern Joint Computer Conference*, (Washington, Dec. 11–13, 1957). New York: Institute of Electrical Engineers.

18. Harel, D., H. Lachover, A. Naamad, A. Pnueli, M. Politi, R. Sherman, A. Shtul-Trauring, "Statemate: A working environment for the development of complex reactive systems," *IEEE Trans. on SE*, **16,** 4 (1990), pp. 403–444.

19. Jones, C., *Assessment and Control of Software Risks*. Englewood Cliffs, N.J.: Prentice-Hall, 1994. p. 619.

20. Coqui, H., "Corporate survival: The software dimension," *Focus '89*, Cannes, 1989.

21. Coggins, James M., "Designing C + + libraries," *C + + Journal*, **1,** 1 (June, 1990), pp. 25–32.

22. The tense is future; I know of no such result yet reported for a fifth use.

23. Jones, op. cit., p 604.

24. Huang, Weigiao, "Industrializing software production," *Proceedings ACM 1988 Computer Science Conference*, Atlanta, 1988. I fear the lack of personal job growth in such an arrangement.

25. The entire September, 1994 issue of *IEEE Software* is on reuse.

26. Jones, op. cit., p. 323.

27. Jones, op. cit., p. 329.

28. Yourdon, E., *Decline and Fall of the American Programmer*. Englewood Cliffs, N.J.: Yourdon Press, 1992, p. 221.

29. Glass, R. L., "Glass"(column), *System Development*, (January, 1988), pp. 4–5.

Chapter 18

1. Boehm, B. W., *Software Engineering Economics,* Englewood Cliffs, N.J.: Prentice-Hall, 1981, pp. 81–84.

2. McCarthy, J., "21 Rules for Delivering Great Software on Time," Software World USA Conference, Washington (Sept., 1994).

Chapter 19

Material quoted without citation is from personal communications.

1. On this painful subject, see also Niklaus Wirth "A plea for lean software," *Computer,* **28,** 2 (Feb., 1995), pp. 64–68.

2. Coleman, D., 1994, "Word 6.0 packs in features; update slowed by baggage," *MacWeek,* **8,** 38 (Sept. 26, 1994), p. 1.

3. Many surveys of machine language and programming language command frequencies *after* fielding have been published. For example, see J. Hennessy and D. Patterson, *Computer Architecture.* These frequency data are very useful for building successor products, although they never exactly apply. I know of no published frequency estimates prepared *before* the product was designed, much less comparisons of *a priori* estimates and *a posteriori* data. Ken Brooks suggests that bulletin boards on the Internet now provide a cheap method of soliciting data from prospective users of a new product, even though only a self-selected set responds.

4. Conklin, J., and M. Begeman, "gIBIS: A Hypertext Tool for Exploratory Policy Discussion," *ACM Transactions on Office Information Systems,* Oct. 1988, pp. 303–331.

5. Englebart, D., and W. English, "A research center for augmenting human intellect," *AFIPS Conference Proceedings, Fall Joint Computer Conference,* San Francisco (Dec. 9–11, 1968), pp. 395–410.

6. Apple Computer, Inc., *Macintosh Human Interface Guidelines,* Reading, Mass.: Addison-Wesley, 1992.

7. It appears the Apple Desk Top Bus could handle two mice electronically, but the operating system provides no such function.

8. Royce, W. W., 1970. "Managing the development of large software systems: Concepts and techniques," *Proceedings, WESCON* (Aug., 1970), reprinted in the *ICSE 9 Proceedings*. Neither Royce nor others believed one could go through the software process without revising earlier documents; the model was put forth as an ideal and a conceptual aid. See D. L. Parnas and P. C. Clements, "A rational design process: How and why to fake it," *IEEE Transactions on Software Engineering*, **SE-12,** 2 (Feb., 1986), pp. 251–257.

9. A major reworking of DOD-STD-2167 produced DOD-STD-2167A (1988), which allows but does not mandate more recent models such as the spiral model. Unfortunately, the MILSPECS that 2167A references and the illustrative examples it uses are still waterfall-oriented, so most procurements have continued to use the waterfall, Boehm reports. A Defense Science Board Task Force under Larry Druffel and George Heilmeyer, in their 1994 "Report of the DSB task force on acquiring defense software commercially," has advocated the wholesale use of more modern models.

10. Mills, H. D., "Top-down programming in large systems," in *Debugging Techniques in Large Systems*, R. Rustin, ed. Englewood Cliffs, N.J.: Prentice-Hall, 1971.

11. Parnas, D. L., "On the design and development of program families," *IEEE Trans. on Software Engineering*, **SE-2,** 1 (March, 1976), pp. 1–9; Parnas, D. L., "Designing software for ease of extension and contraction," *IEEE Trans. on Software Engineering*, **SE-5,** 2 (March, 1979), pp. 128–138.

12. D. Harel, "Biting the silver bullet," *Computer* (Jan., 1992), pp. 8–20.

13. The seminal papers on information hiding are: Parnas, D. L., "Information distribution aspects of design methodology," Carnegie-Mellon, Dept. of Computer Science, Tech-

nical Report (Feb., 1971); Parnas, D. L., "A technique for software module specification with examples," *Comm. ACM*, **5,** 5 (May, 1972), pp. 330–336; Parnas, D. L. (1972). "On the criteria to be used in decomposing systems into modules," *Comm. ACM*, **5,** 12 (Dec., 1972), pp. 1053–1058.

14. The ideas of objects were initially sketched by Hoare and Dijkstra, but the first and most influential development of them was the Simula-67 language by Dahl and Nygaard.

15. Boehm, B. W., *Software Engineering Economics*, Englewood Cliffs, N.J.: Prentice-Hall, 1981, pp. 83–94; 470–472.

16. Abdel-Hamid, T., and S. Madnick, *Software Project Dynamics: An Integrated Approach*, ch. 19, "Model enhancement and Brooks's law." Englewood Cliffs, N.J.: Prentice Hall, 1991.

17. Stutzke, R. D., "A Mathematical Expression of Brooks's Law." In *Ninth International Forum on COCOMO and Cost Modeling*. Los Angeles: 1994.

18. DeMarco, T., and T. Lister, *Peopleware: Productive Projects and Teams*. New York: Dorset House, 1987.

19. Pius XI, Encyclical *Quadragesimo Anno*, [Ihm, Claudia Carlen, ed., *The Papal Encyclicals 1903–1939*, Raleigh, N.C.: McGrath, p. 428.]

20. Schumacher, E. F., *Small Is Beautiful: Economics as if People Mattered*, Perennial Library Edition. New York: Harper and Row, 1973, p. 244.

21. Schumacher, op. cit., p. 34.

22. A thought-provoking wall poster proclaims: "Freedom of the press belongs to him who has one."

23. Bush, V., "That we may think," *Atlantic Monthly*, **176,** 1 (April, 1945), pp. 101–108.

24. Ken Thompson of Bell Labs, inventor of Unix, realized early the importance of big screens for programming. He devised a way to get 120 lines of code, in two columns, onto his primitive Tektronix electron-storage tube. He clung to this terminal through a whole generation of small-window, fast tubes.

Index

Abdel-Hamid, T., 308
abstract data type, 188, 220,
  273
accident, **179**, **182**, 209, 214, 272,
  280, 281, 303, *viii*
accounting, 132
Ada, **188**, 283
administrator, 33
Adobe Photoshop, 281
advancement, dual ladder of,
  119, 242
advisor, testing, 192
Aiken, H. H., 291
airplane-seat metaphor, 194
Algol, 34, 44, 64, 68, 203, 295,
  302
algorithm, **102**, 239
allocation, dynamic memory, 57
alpha test, 142, 245, 266
alpha version, 240
Alto personal workstation, 260
ANSI, 168, 249
APL, 64, 98, 136, 175, 203, 302
Apple Computer, Inc., 264, 306
Apple Desk Top Bus, 307
Apple Lisa, 260
Apple Macintosh, 255, 258, **264**,
  284, 291, 306

AppleScript, 287
architect, 37, **41**, 54, 62, 66, 79,
  100, 233, 236, 238, **255**, 257
architecture, **44**, 143, 233, 234,
  245, 266
archive, chronological, 33
aristocracy, 39, 44, 46
Aristotle, 209, 303
Aron, J., 90, 93, 237, 297
ARPA network, 78
artificial intelligence, **190**, 302
assembler, 132
authority, 8, 80, 231, 236
AutoCad, 285
AutoLisp, 285
automatic programming, 302

Bach, J. S., 47
Backus, J. W., 64, 295
Backus-Naur Form, 64
Baker, F. T., 36, 294, 300
Balzer, R., 302
Bardain, E. F., 296
barrier, sociological, 119
Begeman, M., 306
Belady, L., 122, 123, 150, 243,
  246, 298, 301
Bell Northern Research, 270

Note: Bold numerals indicate a relatively substantial discussion of a topic.